FAMINE

Previous Books by Dr. Cahill

Health on the Horn of Africa
Tropical Medicine in Temperate Climates
The Untapped Resource: Medicine and Diplomacy
Health and Development
Teaching Tropical Medicine
Clinical Tropical Medicine—Vol. I
Clinical Tropical Medicine—Vol. II
Medical Advice for the Traveler
Tropical Medicine: A Handbook for Practitioners
Health in New York State
Somalia: A Perspective
Irish Essays
Threads for a Tapestry

FAMINE

Edited by
Kevin M. Cahill, M.D.

ORBIS BOOKS
Maryknoll, New York 10545

The Catholic Foreign Mission Society of America (Maryknoll) recruits and trains people for overseas missionary service. Through Orbis Books Maryknoll aims to foster the international dialogue that is essential to mission. The books published, however, reflect the opinions of their authors and are not meant to represent the official position of the society.

Library of Congress Cataloging in Publication Data

Main entry under title:

Famine.

   Includes bibliographical references.
   1. Famines—Addresses, essays, lectures.
2. Food relief—Addresses, essays, lectures.
3. Food supply—Addresses, essays, lectures.
I. Cahill, Kevin M.
HC79.F3F35   363.8   81-19034
ISBN 0-88344-133-0   AACR2
ISBN 0-88344-132-2 (pbk.)

For Paul and Helen Hamlyn,
who feed my soul

CONTENTS

ACKNOWLEDGEMENTS

The Symposium that was the basis for this book was the twelfth in a series of such programs sponsored by the Tropical Disease Center of Lenox Hill Hospital.

Generous grants from the Fannie E. Rippel Foundation and the Hoffmann La-Roche Foundation helped defray some of the symposium expenses. Bill Hanlon and Elizabeth Higgins graciously—and expertly—helped me edit this text. My syntax and grammar were corrected by Leonard Bernstein with his usual generosity. Every aspect of the production of *Famine* by Orbis Books has been under the wise and gentle direction of Philip Scharper, whose views on philosophy, theology, and the English language have influenced me since student days.

INTRODUCTION

Though blood may flow in both, there is a clear difference between a minor laceration and a hemorrhage. So too we must not confuse undernutrition or even hunger with famine. Famine is of a different scale, reflecting a prolonged total shortage of foods, in a limited geographic area, and leads to widespread disease and death from starvation.

Famines have occurred in all areas of the globe and in every period of recorded history. But the era in which we live has the odious distinction of being the period when more people will die of famine than in any previous century. To fully appreciate this indictment it is necessary to review the traditional causes of famine, and then to realize that today mass death by starvation is rarely due to the vagaries of nature but reflects, rather, human decisions. Today's famines are man-made, for we have the ability to control short-term food deficits.

Many factors can cause a local crop failure—droughts, floods, locusts, the spread of the desert, toxins, the erosion or exhaustion of soil—but in our modern world of instant communications and rapid transport there must almost be a calculated effort for famine to flourish. There must be a failure of the social system and a denial of our obligation to share. Political decisions—or indecisions—ignorance, neglect, economic and cultural conflicts cause famine today.

Since we, in the developed nations, control the critical surplus food supplies of the world, and have the capacity to both make and resolve or, as is too often the case, ignore famines, it is most appropriate that we reflect carefully on the history, economics, reality, ethics, and response to famine. Eighty percent of the earth's population live in the developing nations of the Third World where the specter of famine is ever present. It is for them—and for our children—that I planned this book on famine.

1

PART I

The History of Famine

In approaching a topic as complex and emotional as famine a proper perspective is essential. In choosing a scholar who could review the history of famines throughout the ages I also sought one who would bring a view that comes only from personal involvement in starvation situations.

Professor Dennis G. Carlson teaches International Health as well as the History of Medicine at the Johns Hopkins School of Public Health. More importantly, from my point of view, he has studied famine first hand during several years' service in Ethiopia, and this formative experience is reflected in his chapter.

1

FAMINE IN HISTORY:
WITH A COMPARISON OF TWO MODERN
ETHIOPIAN DISASTERS

Dennis G. Carlson

Those who are hungry have no need of an elaborate philosophy to stimulate or excuse discontent. . . . The good is enough to eat and the rest is talk.[1]

—*Bertrand Russell*

History documents the fact that famine has been a frequent, significant threat to humankind. Lack of food due to natural and man-made disasters has killed millions of people, weakened communities and states, and destroyed powerful empires and civilizations. In almost every agricultural area of the globe, crops have failed because of drought, flood, freezing, pests, disease, war, or mismanagement of resources. Despite improvements in agriculture and transportation, acute and chronic food shortages are increasing in both industrialized and nonindustrialized parts of the world. Because the distribution of resources is so markedly uneven, and because cultural patterns and political organizations differ so widely, historical experience can be useful in learning how a variety of people and governments have responded to these life-threatening times. This study will first give a brief overview of the prevalence, causes, and impact of famines throughout history, and then will attempt to highlight some contrasting reactions in two specific situations and search for clues for more effective responses.

One of the earliest records of this type of human disaster is written on the Stele of Famine, found in a tomb in the first cataract of the Nile. It describes the havoc of famine in Egypt about 5,000 years ago:

Dennis G. Carlson is associate professor, Department of International Health, John Hopkins University.

5

I am in mourning on my high throne for the vast misfortune, because the Nile flood in my time has not come for seven years! Light is the grain; there is lack of crops and of all kinds of food. Each man has become a thief to his neighbor. They desire to hasten and cannot walk. The child cries, the youth creeps along, and the old man falters; their souls are bowed down, their legs are bent together and drag along the ground, and their hands rest in their bosoms. The counsel of the great ones in the court is but emptiness. Torn open are the chests of provisions, but instead of contents there is air. Everything is exhausted.[2]

Similar accounts can be obtained from nearly every society with recorded history. Egypt, Greece, and Rome experienced major famines, as did the civilizations of the Middle and Far East. India withstood dozens of famines every century for at least four millennia. China is reported to have had 1,800 famines, in local or widespread areas, between 108 B.C. and A.D. 1911.[3] Continental Europe and Russia had frequent famines, and the British Isles had dozens of famines under Roman, Saxon, Anglo-Saxon, and Norman occupations, as well as in more recent centuries.[4] The Ethiopians at the headwaters of the Blue Nile weathered about ten major famines per century.[5] In sub-Saharan Africa, famines are frequent, almost regular occurrences in the arid and semi-arid zones. During the 1979 census in Kenya, census takers developed a list of major events to pinpoint dates of births and deaths in interviewing nonliterate people in a semi-arid area. Of the thirty events known to many people during the past hundred years, fifteen were famines or occurrences relating directly to inadequate food supplies.[6]

There are fewer recorded instances of food depletion described in the New World, although it is known that native American cultures suffered major droughts and famines during the thirteenth century, disrupting an advanced agricultural economy.[7] It is also well recorded that European settlers in the seventeenth century in North America experienced severe food shortages, as illustrated by the early Thanksgiving celebrations.

That our history books give surprisingly little emphasis to the impact of famine on social, economic, political, and medical development is curious and probably significant. There is no disputing, however, that famine has been a widely prevalent and important phenomenon.

Famine has both natural and artificial causes. Drought or a relative lack of rain is the most important natural cause; the lack of regular rainfall may extend for several years or even decades, as the climatic pattern begins a progressively drier trend. Famine can also come after flooding which destroys seeds and plants; Europe and the Indian subcontinent have been prone to that problem. A third category of natural causes is insect infestation or infections. A fungus epidemic is thought to have caused the Irish Potato Famine of 1845–1848. Rinderpest, an epidemic disease of cattle, spread its devastation of herds, causing famine throughout eastern, central, and southern Africa for a decade or more. Huge locust swarms have frequently destroyed grain crops, causing famine.

War is a major artificial, or man-made cause of disrupted and inadequate food supplies. Normal agriculture is disrupted; armies commandeer or loot stores of grain and other foodstuffs, as in Greece and the Netherlands during the German occupation in World War II; supply lines are cut; occasionally urban populations are caught in a siege, planned or unplanned, as in Warsaw and Leningrad during World War II; and prisoners frequently suffer famine conditions in concentration camps and prisons.[8]

Governments can, however, even in peacetime, contribute to serious food shortages by action or inaction. Difficult as it is to comprehend, many countries continue to export foodstuffs even when famine conditions exist at home. In Roman times, British grain was sent to Rome despite shortages for the local populace. Even sovereign independent nations like Ethiopia under Haile Selassie I exported grain in the early 1970s while serious drought and famine were present. The need for foreign exchange is cited as a reason for this practice sometimes, and careless management or corruption by privileged persons is often a real factor.

It is not possible to gather accurate statistics during the chaos of famine conditions. Nevertheless, efforts are usually made to estimate the number of lives lost during these terrifying periods. Probably the most costly famine in terms of human lives in history was in 1876–1879 in North China, when approximately nine to thirteen million people died following three years of drought. Relief from outside was hindered by rough terrain, reluctance of officials to accept aid, and attacks by starving bands of Chinese on the columns of relief supplies. China also had other major famines, among them those of 1333–1337, 1892–1894, and 1920–1921.[9]

India underwent at least twelve catastrophic famines in the three hundred years from 1630 to 1944 (1630, 1769–1770, 1790–1792, 1803–1804, 1837–1838, 1866–1870, 1869–1870, 1873, 1876–1878, 1896–1897, 1899–1900, and 1943–1944), with estimated deaths ranging from 1.25 to five million persons during each period. Russia had a serious famine in 1891–1892 and two more major famines beginning in 1921 and 1932, with 1.25 to five million estimated deaths each time. Ireland suffered one million deaths out of a population of eight million from 1846 to 1848, and another million people emigrated.[10]

Major famines have occurred repeatedly in Africa in the past thirty years. Ethiopia has suffered repeated local and generalized droughts; the Republic of the Congo had famine during the civil war following independence; in Nigeria, during the civil war from 1967 to 1969, perhaps one million deaths occurred; the Sahel famine from 1965 to 1974 claimed the lives of several hundred thousand people.[11]

Famine usually happens when many elements of the biological and social ecosystems have been profoundly disturbed and altered. The human physical stigmata are well known: wasting, emaciation, and edema. Psychological effects are less obvious but important: after an initial period of increased activity and agitation, a general apathy and lethargy prevails, with loss of interest in normal human concerns except for finding food. Interpersonal relationships may be broken down so completely that parents devour their own children; cannibalism has been reported during famine times in almost every part of the world, although apparently less frequently in China and India.[12] Infants, children, and the elderly suffer first; young and middle-aged adults are usually able to travel to food sources, leaving the young and the old to fend for themselves and possibly die. The animal world can also become ravenously hungry and leave their usual habitats to encroach upon human territory in towns and cities; animals may attack humans in broad daylight without apparent fear.

Social chaos is evident everywhere, as refugees flock to cities or roads seeking food. Almost all normal functions are reduced or halted. Economic confusion is pronounced, as hoarding occurs, and costs of staple foods rocket to three, five, or one hundred times the normal price. Paradoxically, in moderate famine times the price of animals may fall, when farmers sell their cows, oxen, sheep, and goats to buy cereals, and merchants may accumulate enormous profits. Rationing and price controls are often difficult to enforce amidst active black markets. Food shortages have the most severe impact on the lower economic classes, less on the advantaged. In a time of famine, the urban working classes and those on low government salaries are often the first and most severely hit, because their fixed wages and salaries do not keep pace with grossly inflated food prices.

Famine has been a threat to political control and national stability throughout history. Egyptian rulers established control of the cereal crops from about 2000 B.C. and struggled to maintain a steady minimal food supply to the urban dwellers despite fluctuations in production relating to variations in the Nile floodwater volume.[13] In the fourteenth to sixteenth centuries A.D., when food riots broke out and threatened to topple the government, desperate administrators strove to establish stable prices and a continuous survival ration of grain and bread.[14]

Rome in its powerful centuries depended on grain supplied from all over the Empire. With a large nonproductive urban population in Rome, that capital city particularly depended on food from Egypt and the North African colonies. Imperial leaders were acutely conscious of this dependence and often paid a heavy military and political price to maintain regular shipments of cereals. Often the citizens of Rome ate while the Egyptian populace went hungry. Usually imperial administrators were able to rely on the maxim, "A well-fed army is a loyal one," but even that principle did not always hold true, because armies did sometimes revolt. Opposing rulers like Philip the Arab also were able to weaken Roman control by the tactic of interfering with the military food supply lines.[15]

In fact, according to some recent conclusions by Weitz, the decline of the Roman Empire in the third century A.D. was in large measure due to famine conditions and epidemics of plague. Crops repeatedly failed due to drought, and the malnourished populace was then more susceptible to infectious diseases. The civil disorders in Egypt during Roman rule were a response to a food shortage and also contributed to the deterioration of the irrigation system. The chain of reactions continued in Rome as food supplies diminished, and the Roman citizens rioted for bread. Much arable land was uncultivated due to a lack of labor; occasionally attempts were made to force soldiers to do farm labor, but rebellions followed. With all these disruptive happenings, the population of the Roman Empire decreased from 70 million to 50 million by the end of the third century.[16]

Inability to maintain food supplies was a major factor not only for the Roman Empire's decline, but in other societies as well. The ancient societies of Mohenjo-Daro and Harrappas in the Indus Valley allegedly declined in significant response to famine conditions, as did the ancient kingdoms of Ghana and Mali.[17]

Individuals and governments have responded differently to famine, even within specific communities and historical periods. The political and cosmological views of affected people have important influences. One of the most strikingly predictable responses by government officials has been to deny and suppress famine reports as long as possible. Not only the top echelons ignore, deny, or become angry with allegations of food shortages; all down the line, appointed officials and civil servants work hard to belittle the seriousness of the matter. This can be explained in several ways. The reality of people starving is extremely difficult for anyone to bear emotionally. Some explain that semi-starvation is a "normal" or "natural" way of life for certain populations. Often information is woefully inadequate, and responsible people are not fully informed. Perhaps most important, government officials feel that famine conditions indicate somehow that they have not properly performed their public roles. They are faced with actual or potential loss of power, as an individual, a party, or a government. This last possibility is very real, and like death, is often easier to deny than to face.

In order to understand more concretely and comprehensively the impact of these patterns and principles on human lives, I would like to turn our attention to the story of one country, Ethiopia, which has struggled with a lack of adequate food for millennia and has had thirty major famines during the past five centuries. In particular, I would like to analyze and compare two devastating famine periods during the past century which have profoundly influenced the course of social and political events, the Great Famine of 1888–1892, and the Long Famine of 1965–1974. These two disasters illustrate similar facets while also presenting striking differences which underline the need to consider each famine as a unique event.

The Great Famine of 1888–1892 began one year after an unusually hot and dry year in the Horn of Africa.[18] The Italians were making a belated effort to get into the European scramble for Africa and had established a foothold on the highlands of Eritrea, the northern part of present-day Ethiopia. As part of their military buildup in the fall of 1888, they imported cattle from India and Italy. Apparently a virulent strain of the rinderpest virus infected some of the Indian herds, which were brought to the Red Sea coastal town of Massawa, subsequently infecting indigenous animals. The disease spread like wildfire, and combined with the limited grazing food and relative malnutrition due to the previous year of high temperatures and low rainfall, the rinderpest quickly decimated flocks in the area. By January 1889, the cattle plague had spread to the central highlands, and within six months the disease had extended throughout the whole country. Hardly any cattle survived in all of Ethiopia except at high elevations in a few scattered mountain areas in Gojjam. The fact that the drought continued for three more years is important, but the crippling blow was that no oxen were left for plowing and harvesting, essential in traditional agricultural practice. The peasant population became almost completely discouraged with the loss of the means to their livelihood, and then the diseases of famine exploded—dysentery, tuberculosis, edema, and a virulent strain of smallpox. Human mortality was estimated at 15 to 20 percent of the country's approximately eight million people; some local areas suffered a 50 percent loss of life. Some cannibalism was reported. Hyenas, lions, leopards, and wild dogs invaded villages and towns to attack humans. The price of animals increased 40 times; the price of cereals, when available, increased 100 times, and seed grain was used for human food. Community and social life was completely disrupted, with able-bodied people flooding the cities and towns. This poem, written in 1890, pours out the sorrow and desperation of the Ethiopian in those days:

> Not with a strong ox or a sharp plow
> Do we till our fields today;
> We work our land with our naked hand
> Imploring the grace of an angry God
> As we bend to our barren toil.
>
> The sun arose and climbed in the sky
> And we dug the soil in vain—
> Old men, green youths, and even young girls;
> But our labor was fruitless still.
> They sowed the field not with golden grain
> For dear friends and hated enemies were lying there;
> And instead of young plants on the undulating plain
> Tombstones were erected.
>
> The fields do not give the expected crop.
> Only cotton is born in the valley,
> But no one gathers its fruit;
> The wind of the desert scatters it down.
> It is a long time since my clothes were torn,

Will no one weave me some more?
No one replies to me now.
What shall I do? Is this not poverty?
I shall clothe myself in the humid earth.[19]

Ethiopia's enemies were pressing on the west as well as the north. Sudanese Dervishes were attacking west of Gondar at Mettema. On March 10, 1889, Emperor Yohannes IV died in battle and left the Empire without unified leadership. Menelik of Showa emerged within a few months and was crowned as the new emperor in November with a bare minimum of celebration and fanfare. There was no royal feasting in Addis Ababa, as the famine was hitting its peak. Emperor Menelik opened his own granary to feed the starving refugees and sent emissaries abroad to purchase food. None of the relief supplies reached the Ethiopian highlands, for the Danakil people of the lowlands were also suffering starvation, and they intercepted all food shipments. Menelik urged the people to pray and cultivate what they could by hand. He set a personal example by going daily to the fields and digging with a hoe, and by attending public prayers.

The Emperor had other worries too. Just before Emperor Yohannes had been killed, the Italian envoy to Addis Ababa had sent a message to Rome saying that all Ethiopia is threatened by a famine and economic dislocation:

In this state of things Italy should not be apprehensive about difficulties for possessions in the Red Sea in general or for Massawa in particular. . . . On the contrary, one must not allow this favorable moment to pass. We cannot fall into the error of giving Tigray time to reorganize and refortify itself.[20]

Even before Menelik was crowned, the Italians pressed their invasion plans and moved southward through Eritrea and began pushing into the next province, Tigray. Although there was almost no armed resistance, the famine conditions bogged the invaders' progress down, for they could not rely on local food sources, and the supply lines became extremely long and difficult to maintain.

The rains returned after 1892, and the Ethiopian economy and society began to mend. Menelik himself was expanding his own empire to the south and west. Menelik also began preparations to battle the Italian forces and to drive them out if possible. On March 1, 1896, an Italian army of 20,000 troops with superior artillery was routed by the Ethiopians. Two-thirds of the Italians were killed or captured. Europe was shocked that an African army had defeated a Western army so decisively, and Italy became the laughingstock of the colonial powers.[21] This humiliation would serve as motivation for the Italians' second attempt at colonizing Ethiopia in 1935. Drought, rinderpest, and famine were door openers to outside enemy forces in 1888, but in the future, the political danger would be from within.

In the twentieth century, Ethiopia experienced four major famine periods. In addition, there have been many local and regional drought times when food scarcity became serious for people living in a particular area. The population was growing at about a 2.5 percent annual rate, so that between 1958 and 1980 the population increased from about 15 million to approximately 26 million. In the mid-1960s the dessication trend began across the Sahel in west and central Africa, and Ethiopia also experienced several years of low rainfall and regional famine conditions in the northern and eastern parts of the country. By 1965, large numbers of refugees from Wollo and Tigray began flooding into towns and cities and gathering along main roads leading north and south, where they hoped to find food, employment, or other relief. An estimated 150,000 people died from starvation and related diseases in a three-year period, and four to six million people were living under famine conditions. Cholera and severe dysenteries were common, and tuberculosis and pneumonia spread rapidly among the malnourished refugees and those left behind.[22]

Famine relief activities were disorganized and desultory in 1965 and 1966. A small amount of international assistance was received, but the Ethiopian government did little to provide services or generate external help. The Ministry of Health sent some special teams to highway centers to treat the sick, to help manage food distribution, and to organize environmental sanitation, which was an enormous problem when hundreds of people were ill with dysentery in temporary accommodations.

People in one refugee settlement near Lake Tana were interviewed about the events which had taken place and how they understood what had happened. All their domesticated animals had died or been eaten. Most people had left parents and older relatives at home. Fewer than half expected to return to their home area. Sixty percent had obtained temporary work in the host community. Seventy-five percent believed that the famine was either God's punishment or that God knew the reason why it happened. A passive, fatalistic worldview predominated, particularly in the areas hardest hit by drought.[23]

The rainfall improved somewhat in 1967, 1968, and 1969, but the environment and population were only partially recovering in 1970 when another drought period began to parch the north, east, and southern areas of Ethiopia. This dryness continued for almost eight years, with only minor temporary improvement over most of the country. The government of Emperor Haile Selassie I suppressed all news of the serious famine conditions in Ethiopia to outsiders; the national media had only minor reporting with some allusions to a need for relief efforts. Officials of bilateral and multilateral government agencies were ordered not to report any famine news. Ethiopian university students and faculty sensed the need and raised a fund of about $15,000 in U.S. currency. When they attempted to present their help in the Wollo Province, perhaps the area hardest hit, the local governor denied the presence of famine, refused their proffered gift, and sent them back to Addis Ababa. Soon after, a student-led riot broke out in the capital of Wollo, and seven high-school students were killed. The government handling of the famine quickly became a national political issue, even while the world at large knew little of what was happening.

In the fall of 1973, reports finally reached Europe of the true situation. An officer of UNICEF, Steven Green, actively facilitated awareness of the famine in the diplomatic circles of Addis Ababa and soon the seriousness of the situation was reported widely in Europe. Belatedly the Emperor mounted an international appeal, sending official emissaries to Europe and North America requesting help. The price of cereals doubled and trebled around the country, making it extremely difficult for workers on set wages and low salaries to buy food. Unrest began in the most dangerous place, from the government's viewpoint: in the northern military frontier area. Ethiopia was trying to quell antigovernment forces in Eritrea, and another army was dealing with Somali incursions into the Ogaden at the opposite end of the Empire, in the southeast. Further trouble occurred when enlisted troops in the north refused to fight because their salaries could not provide food for themselves and their families. The Emperor ordered their salaries increased by 50 percent, but even that addition was insufficient, and the soldiers continued to rebel. A delegation of high-ranking officers was sent to the trouble spot, and they were promptly seized and held by the rebellious garrison.

At about the same time, a similar situation was occurring at the southern frontier in the Ogaden and also in yet another area, Neghelli, in Sidamo, where both food and water were in extremely short supply. Before national authorities knew what was happening, a demand was made in February 1974 by military spokesmen that the Emperor form a new government, which he felt forced to attempt. An unplanned revolution proceeded, as the Emperor's efforts proved inadequate, and a nationwide council of enlisted men and low-ranking military officers took over power. By September 1974, Emperor Haile Selassie I was formally deposed and humiliated by being transported out of town in a dilapidated Volkswagen.[24]

The trigger for this violent, radical change of power was the government's mismanagement of famine conditions. This became one key test by which members of the Emperor's government were subsequently tried by courts of inquiry set up after the new regime had control. Few high-ranking officials were judged not guilty, and about sixty senior authorities were executed at the end of October 1974.

The drought continued in many parts of the country until 1977. In internationally published interviews, ethnic Somalis who had lived in the Ethiopian part of the Ogaden stated that a major reason they did not remain loyal to Ethiopia was that their people had not been served adequately in famine relief. After 1977, food production did begin to improve, and a program of food relief was generally successful, but food prices are still relatively high in 1981, and famine conditions continue in the war zones of the north and southeast. International relief efforts are still in effect, but the food supply apparently is significantly improved in comparison with the early and mid-1970s.

Let us look at important similarities in these two major famine periods in recent Ethiopian history: hundreds of thousands of people died because of lack of food and closely associated illnesses in both of the periods; social, economic, and political chaos erupted both times, and major changes in internal and external power relationships occurred. Both events illustrate how tenuous is the ecological balance which exists despite the external appearance of stability of the biophysical and social orders. During both famines, a traditional worldview was expressed in which drought and famine were believed by a large part of the population to be part of the judgment and punishment of God for human sin, with a sense that little could be done to avert or minimize such divine action. (This attitude was not limited to the Ethiopian peasants. In early 1974, an expatriate said during a national conference on the famine that he believed God was trying to teach the nation by means of the famine.) The inseparable interrelationships of climate, food, economics, disease, social organization, and culture were again clearly demonstrated.

There are important contrasts between the two famines as well. The Great Famine of 1888–1892 was caused by a combination of drought and the rinderpest cattle epidemic. The economic dislocations were less severe in the Long Famine of the 1960s and 1970s because of closer linkages to the world markets and improved transportation systems. Perhaps because he had just come into power in 1889, Emperor Menelik did not try to hide the facts about Ethiopia's desperate food shortage. Haile Selassie's government unconscionably refused to inform the international community of the scope and degree of the disaster which was devastating the country. And last, in the most recent famine, the political hazards proved more dangerous from within than from outside the country.

Looking more generally at famines in human history, we can draw some further conclusions useful for consideration by informed citizens, politicians, public officials, scholars, business people, military leaders, and all those working for the public good.

1. Famines on a large and small scale have been almost constant in the experience of human societies. Plans can and must be made to deal with these events, which are almost certain to be recurrent.
2. Although drought has been and still is the most important single cause of famine, other natural and man-made causes can initiate or contribute to famine progression. These processes must be understood more fully from several analytical viewpoints.
3. Famine conditions usually mean that the total ecosystem—physical, biological, social, and economic—is profoundly shaken.
4. No single professional group or discipline or sector of society can be given sole responsibility for analyzing, preventing, or managing famine situations. No dimension of life can escape the impact of famines when they occur. Interdependent collaboration is mandatory.[25]
5. Famine conditions pose special challenges for the political order. Internal

and external threats are particularly dangerous in times of food shortage and economic flux.

6. Famines, although sometimes localized, are often regional in scale, spreading beyond national boundaries. This poses special problems when political conflicts and tensions exist. The Ethiopian poet in 1890 summarized this truth when he said,

> While the cruel famine, like the Gallas, destroys the people,
> There is no one who can make peace.[26]

7. The worldviews, beliefs, and value systems of leaders and the body politic have obvious and subtle influence upon the responses made to famine. These need to be recognized and accommodated.

A number of questions remain which have not been adequately addressed and which merit further study.

1. What are the relationships of famine (particularly an acute epidemic food shortage) to long-term or chronic undernutrition for populations of people? In what ways are they quite separate? In what ways are they closely connected?[27]
2. How can the influence of political ideological differences be reduced to contribute to good nutrition for all people, whatever their class, ethnicity, or economic situation?

These questions are enormously complex and difficult, but they are among the most crucial issues humanity faces today.

NOTES

1. Bertrand Russell, *A History of Western Philosophy,* Part II (1945). Cited in Ancel Keys, Josef Brozek, Austin Henschel, Olaf Mickelson, and Henry Longstreet Taylor, *The Biology of Human Starvation* (Minneapolis: University of Minnesota Press, 1950).

2. Ibid., p. 5.

3. James Cornell, *The Great International Disaster Book* (New York: Scribners, 1976), p. 132.

4. Cornelius Walford, *The Famines of the World, Past and Present* (1879), Research and Source Works Series, n. 556 (New York: B. Franklin, 1970 Papers of the Statistical Society of London, 1879).

5. Richard Pankhurst, *Introduction to the Economic History of Ethiopia* (London, 1961, and New York: Humanities, 1961), pp. 238–240.

6. Government of Kenya, *1979 Census Report.*

7. Cornell, *Disaster Book*, p. 221.

8. W. H. Adolph, "Nutrition in Internment Camps in the Far East," *Nutrition Review* 2 (1944): 193–196.

9. Cornell, *Disaster Book*, p. 133. See also *Encyclopedia Britannica*, Vol. 9 (Chicago: William Benton, 1963), pp. 63–64.

10. Cornell, *Disaster Book*, pp. 133–134.

11. Hal Sheets and Roger Morris, *Disaster in the Desert: Failures of International Relief in the West African Drought* (Washington: Carnegie Endowment for International Peace, 1974).

12. Keys, *Biology of Starvation*, p. 5.

13. Elizabeth Maxwell pointed out that Genesis 47:13–26 describes how Joseph was Pharaoh's agent in accumulating the land of the Egyptian people for himself during a long famine period. (Personal communication.) This is also described in other sources.

14. Boaz Shoshan, "Grain Riots and the 'Moral Economy': Cairo, 1350–1517," *Journal of Interdisciplinary History* 10 (Winter 1980): 459–478.

15. Daniel Weitz, *Famine and Plague as Factors in the Collapse of the Roman Empire in the Third Century* (Ann Arbor: Universal Microfilms International, 1972), p. 132.

16. Ibid., p. 142.

17. Cornell, *Disaster Book*, p. 221.

18. Richard Pankhurst, "The Great Ethiopian Famine of 1888–1892: A New Assessment," *Journal of the History of Medicine and Allied Sciences* 21 (1966): 95–124, 271–94.

19. Ibid., pp. 115–116. The memory of the 1888–1892 famine is still very much alive in the traditional communities around Gondar in north central Ethiopia. In 1974 Ato Wubineh, Patriarch of Kossogay Medhane Alem, then eighty-seven years old, told me in vivid, intensely emotional terms how his family had been forced to move about foraging for food and fighting off the hyenas and lions. He and his eighty-six-year-old wife talked and argued about it as if it had happened only a year before.

20. Ibid., pp. 291–94.

21. Sven Rubenson, *The Survival of Ethiopian Independence* (London: Heinemann Educational Books, 1976), pp. 399–406.

22. Jack Shepherd, *The Politics of Starvation* (New York, Washington: Carnegie Endowment for International Peace, 1975).

23. Tsegaye Teckle and Dennis G. Carlson. "An Economic and Social Survey of Famine Refugees in Begemidr-Semien Province," *Proceedings of the Public Health Practice Conference* (Gondar, Ethiopia, June 1966).

24. Pankhurst, "Great Ethiopian Famine," fn. 19, p. 116.

25. Gunnar Blix, Yngve Hofanader and Bo Valquist, eds., *Famine: A Symposium Dealing With Nutrition and Relief Operations in Times of Disaster* (Uppsala: Almquist and Wiksells, 1971).

26. Pankhurst, "Great Ethiopian Famine," fn. 19, p. 116.

27. The International Centre for Diarrheal Disease Research in Bangladesh has demonstrated the positive correlation of malnutrition and significantly higher infant mortality rates. In famine periods it is logical to assume that undernourished infants, children, and adults die more frequently. International Centre for Diarrheal Disease Research, Bangladesh, *Special Publication No. 11*, November 1980, p. 21. *Growth and Development Studies*, Mehran, July 1979, *Scientific Report No. 28*, p. 1.

PART II

The Reality of Famine

There is nothing theoretical about famine for those who experience this calamity. Every American reader has seen horror pictures of recent malnutrition victims on television screens, but even those flashing images can not capture the chaos of a refugee camp, or the hopeless torpor that epidemic hunger produces in a once-proud society.

In this section four major famine areas are reviewed. For Cambodia and Somalia men who assumed primary responsibility for dealing with these disasters share their unique experiences. For China and South Asia, there are chapters based on personal perspective and careful analyses which lead also towards a better understanding of the common problems in other famine areas.

2

FAMINE, MEDIA, AND GEO-POLITICS: THE KHMER RELIEF EFFORT OF 1980

Victor H. Palmieri

I

A striking indication of social and technological progress is the fact that famine induced by natural causes is no longer a persistent threat to human life. The development of the international food-security system administered by the UN World Food Program and the Food and Agriculture Organization (FAO) means that, even in the most remote regions, drought, earthquake, or flood are not always now, as they once were, the forerunners of starvation.

Today famine is more likely to result from the cruelties of human beings than the caprices of nature. War and civil strife, guerrilla insurgency and counter-terrorism, search and destroy missions and crop denial tactics—all can have effects on food stocks and food production as devastating as the excesses of nature. The difference is that relief operations are so much more difficult and complicated to conduct in the setting of war or revolution, where political priorities normally prevail over humanitarian concerns. Thus the recent experience with the relief program in war-ravaged Cambodia is worth examining.

There are probably few parallels in recent history to the decade of agony suffered by the little country once called Cambodia, now Kampuchea. After years of war and internal strife, Pol Pot's Khmer Rouge regime took power in 1975, and a new nightmare began for the Khmer people. How many perished under Pol Pot—savagely murdered or simply starved or worked to death—will never be known with certainty; estimates center on two million. Virtually every person with managerial or technical background was eliminated, and all equipment needed for agriculture and industry was systematically destroyed. In addition, the supply of draft animals was almost wiped out by livestock diseases.

Victor H. Palmieri is former Ambassador at Large and U.S. Coordinator of Refugee Affairs.

The holocaust continued until the Vietnamese invasion of December 1978, reducing the capacity of the country to produce sufficient food for itself to a point where famine appeared to be a certainty. With general starvation in sight, thousands of families—villagers and townspeople as well as peasants, some coming from as far as Phnom Penh—began streaming toward the Thai border in search of food and a safe haven. Within a few months there were over 300,000 Khmer in makeshift settlements straddling the border in the area of Aranyaprathet, a Thai town four hours by car from Bangkok. These densely populated shanty towns lacked sanitation facilities of any kind, creating a constant risk of a typhoid or cholera epidemic.

With 15,000 Khmer already in United Nations High Commissioner for Refugees (UNHCR) camps throughout Thailand awaiting third-country re-settlement, in addition to 130,000 Vietnamese and Laotians, these massive concentrations of frightened, hungry people on the border, roaming the countryside foraging for food, water, and firewood and disrupting the local villages, created serious political and security problems for the Thai government headed by Prime Minister Kriangsak. Tensions mounted quickly, and in June 1979, when some 40,000 Khmer crossed into Thailand, they were forcibly expelled by the Thai military, sustaining heavy loss of life in the Vietnamese minefields which lay across their path as they fled into Kampuchea.

This tragic incident created a lasting fear in both the UN and the U.S. government circles of forcible repatriation actions by the Thais. In response, emergency units were established in the State Department in Washington, D.C., and in the U.S. Embassy in Bangkok to coordinate U.S. support for the assistance program and to spur relief activities on the border. From the start, U.S. Ambassador Morton Abramowitz played a key role in mobilizing energy and raising consciousness levels in the State Department bureaucracy and the White House, as well as in the Thai government.

In Phnom Penh, there was great reluctance to permit operations by the UN agencies because of the General Assembly's vote to maintain the credentials of the Pol Pot guerrillas in preference to the Vietnamese-dominated government of Heng Samrin. Finally, in July, after months of negotiations, UNICEF, together with the International Committee of the Red Cross (ICRC), established a base for relief operations in Phnom Penh through the instrumentality of a joint mission. Included in the UN group were the UN High Commissioner for Refugees (UNHCR), the Food and Agriculture Organization (FAO), and the World Food Program (WFP). Chief of Mission John Saunders reported finding one working telephone and hardly any pencils or paper in the government offices when he arrived in the capital. Moreover, cooperation from the overwhelmed and inexperienced local authorities was hard to obtain. Consequently, while preparations commenced immediately for an airlift from Bangkok of emergency medical and food supplies and critically needed logistical equipment—trucks, barges, and cargo-handling gear—and for transport of bulk food commodities by sea, it was not until October that the first shipments arrived. By that time, private agencies such as Oxfam and the American Friends Service Committee, who found it easier to work with local officials because of their "nonpolitical" status, had already set up their own supply and distribution systems.

Meanwhile, the situation on the Thai border was becoming more and more critical. Various private voluntary organizations, which had been operating in Thai villages and refugee camps since 1975, were the first to begin food and medical assistance programs in the border settlements. By August, UNICEF/ICRC, along with the private agencies, had established a medical assistance and food distribution system for these camps as well as a highly effective "human land-bridge" supplying thousands of farmers and traders daily with rice for transport either on foot or by ox-cart back to the villages and towns, most of them traveling to the Battambang region but some as far as 200 km into the countryside.

Responding to heavy pressure from the relief agencies and the U.S. Embassy, Thai authorities in October agreed to permit an additional 100,000 Khmer to cross the border to enter newly-constructed UNHCR holding centers at Sa Keo and Khao I Dang. However, the Thai government insisted that these "new Khmer" be characterized as "displaced persons," i.e., illegal aliens, rather than refugees. This was to make it clear that they were being held for voluntary repatriation instead of being added to Thailand's huge pool of refugees awaiting resettlement in the U.S. and other countries.

Within Kampuchea, at the same time, the food shortage resulting from the destruction of the 1978 rice crop and the severe drought of the spring of 1979 was becoming increasingly acute. By the fall of 1979, international observers were reporting extreme malnutrition, rampant malaria, and soaring death rates among children, the aged, and the sick.

In October, there came a sudden and highly significant breakthrough in terms of the visibility of the crisis. This resulted from visits by Congressional delegations from both the House and Senate to Phnom Penh followed by Mrs. Carter's trip to the Thai border a few months later. These media events attracted intense public interest and focused worldwide attention and concern on the suffering of the Khmer people. The following excerpt from the report of the Senate delegation conveys the sense of urgency that was transmitted to the U.S. public and to the international community:

> Over the past few days, we have witnessed a human tragedy of enormous and unfathomable proportions. Without a massive and prompt international relief effort, the situation will continue to deteriorate. Inside Cambodia today, and in refugee camps located in Thailand near the Cambodian border, hundreds of thousands of Cambodians face death by starvation and disease. The survival of the Khmer race is in jeopardy.

The response has to be seen as a spectacular achievement in international cooperation. Contributions totaled $820 million during the first fifteen months, including the Joint Mission ($500 million); the Soviets and other Eastern Bloc countries ($200 million estimated); and private organizations

($120 million estimated). During this period the U.S. government contribution amounted to $135 million, $66 million of it in Food for Peace commodities.

These resources made it possible to offset a major part of Kampuchea's 1980 food deficit with shipments of over 330,000 metric tons of food along with substantial quantities of rice seed, farming implements, medical supplies, and logistical equipment, including more than 1,000 trucks.

While the major part of the Joint Mission supplies were not moved out of the warehouses in Phnom Penh and Kom Pong Som until March or April (1980), and while larger per capita distributions of these supplies were made to the urban population and to nonagricultural workers—government cadres in particular—the effect was decisive for two reasons: first of all, this aid allowed the authorities to leave the small 1979–1980 rice crop with the farmers for consumption or barter, along with local foods grown around the villages such as maize, manioc, sweet potatoes, fruit, and fish; secondly, the aid was available for distribution at the critical point when the small winter harvest, which sufficed for only about one-third of the country's 1980 subsistance requirement, was exhausted.

By the spring of 1980, as a result of the international assistance as well as the ingenuity and survival skills of the farmers and villagers who remained at home, and despite the lack of trained personnel, communications facilities, fuel, transport equipment, repair depots, roads, etc., the famine had been checked. By the third quarter of the year UNICEF nutrition surveys were showing a major improvement in the condition of the Khmer in the interior as well as in the border concentrations. In October and November surveys based on sampling techniques found that more than 70 percent of the children in sixteen villages in the South and Southeast of the country were in a "very good nutritional state" with only 7.7 percent severely undernourished. Similar results were reported even earlier for the Battambang region.

Throughout the second half of 1980 rice seed provided to the ox-cart brigade at the border or flown into Phnom Penh from Bangkok made it possible for farmers to double the 700,000 hectares committed to rice production the year before (out of 2,400,000 hectares cultivated in previous years), medical teams from various nations finally were admitted by the Phnom Penh authorities after long delays and began working throughout the country, hundreds of schools aided by UNICEF started functioning again, and the shattered nation slowly began to revive.

For the present, starvation no longer threatens, but Kampuchea will be dependent on international food aid for the indefinite future, and pressing needs continue in the areas of health care and agricultural rehabilitation.

II

The emergency assistance provided to Kampuchea will exceed $1 billion by the end of 1981, an investment greater by far than the total resources committed by the international community for relief of famine throughout the rest of the world over the same period. In terms of humanitarian considerations, the threat to the Khmer justified an all-out effort, but there were other humanitarian crises arising from famine and disease and warfare during this period, particularly in Africa—Somalia, the Sudan, and Uganda, for example—which were extremely critical but received vastly lower levels of response. Clearly, there were special factors involved in the Kampuchean situation and it may be instructive to consider some of them.

Media Coverage

The newspaper and television coverage of Mrs. Carter's trip to Thailand to visit the Khmer holding centers in November of 1979 may have been the key factor in creating public and political support for the relief effort and in generating the momentum which brought forty-nine donor countries to the series of pledging conferences that have been convened at regular intervals over the better part of two years.

Accident played a decisive role in this coverage. Only a few days before Mrs. Carter's arrival, the Thais had opened the Sa Keo holding center to some 30,000 Khmer Rouge who had been holed up in the Cardamon Mountains for months, hiding from the Vietnamese forces, without food or medical supplies. Many women and children were involved in the movement to Sa Keo, and by the time they reached the camp, most of them were in an advanced stage of starvation; scores of them died every day during the first weeks there, despite the best efforts of the medical units.

The heartrending sights that she witnessed there affected Mrs. Carter deeply; news photographs of her with the pitifully emaciated children appeared worldwide in print and broadcast media day after day. These photographs became a powerful visual metaphor for the suffering of all the Khmer people. In fact, the condition of those at Khao I Dang and those massed on the border was never as critical as that of the Khmer Rouge at Sa Keo, and there is reason to doubt that malnutrition and disease reached such levels, even in the worst areas of the interior.

The Geneva Conference of July 1979

While the Kampuchean emergency was developing during the spring of 1979, the world's attention was captured by the dramatic and tragic plight of the Vietnamese boat people, mostly ethnic Chinese from the Cholon section of Saigon (now Hochiminhville) who were being "encouraged"—in fact forced—to depart Vietnam in small boats and risk death in the South China Sea. The boat people came ashore by the thousands to find refuge in Thailand, Malaysia, Hong Kong, and Indonesia, and even as far as the Philippines. In the month of May, more than 50,000 reached these countries of first asylum, with the total approaching 200,000 over the next few months. The number who perished en route will never be known.

As the crisis mounted, certain of these countries, threatened by the political and economic impact of this rapidly growing mass of refugees and the prospect of their indefinite stay, began pushing off the boats, forcing them to continue their desperate journey, often without food, water, or sufficient fuel.

These actions catalyzed the diplomatic situation. In July, the international community met under UN auspices in Geneva to condemn the Vietnamese for the life-destroying exodus. To protect the countries of first asylum from the consequences of a permanent refugee presence and to persuade them to continue granting temporary asylum to the boat people (as well as to the land refugees in Thailand), the group of twenty-one participating countries agreed to increase their resettlement quotas of Indochinese substantially. The U.S. led the way by doubling its intake from 7,000 to 14,000 per month.

The Vietnamese in turn, stung by the almost unprecedented level of international criticism emanating from the conference, and doubtless realizing that the mass exodus was having destabilizing effects in the South, announced that they were discontinuing their "facilitated departure" program, provided that other countries would establish "orderly departure" programs for those permitted to leave Vietnam. After many months of difficult negotiations, such programs got under way in 1980.

By the standards of achievement applicable to international gatherings, the Geneva Conference was a spectacular success. The perception of this success generated high morale among the participating governments and created a base for international cooperation in the related crisis in Kampuchea that would otherwise have been much more difficult and time-consuming to construct.

Geo-Politics

Among the geo-political factors in the Kampuchean situation, none was more potent than the newly forged Soviet alignment with the Vietnamese. First of all, it led to substantial food shipments (although much of these consisted of red corn hated by the Khmer) and other kinds of aid from the Soviets and Eastern bloc countries. Much of this arrived earlier than the Joint Mission shipments and was distributed earlier by the Phnom Penh authorities. When unloading facilities and lack of trained manpower at Kom Pong Som harbor proved to be a major bottleneck in the early months of 1980, a force of Soviet stevedores took over and broke up the cargo jam, working for many weeks to set up more efficient cargo-handling procedures.

Second, by providing the Soviets with a major military base at Cam Rahn Bay, the alliance created the specter of Soviet penetration throughout Indo-China and thus brought bi-polar power factors into play in respect to Kampuchea. Third, it gave the Chinese—always eager to teach the Vietnamese a "second lesson"—added reason to support the Khmer Rouge guerrilla insurgency, even though this enormously complicated the relief effort and also, ironically, tended to legitimize the Vietnamese occupation of Kampuchea in the eyes of the Khmer as a guarantee against the return of Pol Pot.

From the standpoint of the U.S., the role of Thailand as the last friendly outpost in Indo-China made the Vietnamese military presence on the Thai border, along with the destabilizing effects of the refugee flows into Thailand, a clear threat to vital American security interests in Southeast Asia. Similarly, the ASEAN states and Japan saw the occupation of Kampuchea, the installation of the puppet regime there, and the announced intent of the Vietnamese to create an Indo-China federation with Kampuchea and Laos, all as decisive steps toward a dangerous hegemony for Indo-China.

These geo-political factors, by magnifying the importance of Kampuchea in the East-West strategic equation, lent powerful impetus to support for the relief program. However, the same factors also led to behavior on both sides which seriously undercut the humanitarian cause.

An example was the situation on the border where the Thais persisted in supporting the Khmer Rouge together with an exotic assortment of other "resistance groups" who maintained an armed presence in the camps straddling the border, directing most of their energies to raiding each other and terrorizing civilians. This activity regularly disrupted food distributions, endangered the lives of relief workers, and led to constant appeals from UNICEF/ICRC officials seeking to persuade the Thai military to establish a secure environment for relief activity.

The Vietnamese continually denounced the situation on the border and retaliated by refusing to permit a motorized "land bridge"—i.e., truck transport of food supplies from Thailand, or an airlift from Bangkok to provincial airports, which could have been even more useful in view of the terrible condition of the roads. To make things more difficult, they also forced relief flights from Bangkok to fly over the Gulf of Thailand to Hochiminhville before heading into Phnom Penh. In June, after broadcasting repeated warnings and condemnations, the Vietnamese main force units crossed the border into Thailand and conducted a brief fire fight with Thai units and the resistance groups before withdrawing. The incursion caused several hundred casualties and scattered thousands more of the Khmer over the countryside on both sides of the border.

The attitude of distrust and suspicion shared by Washington and Bangkok (and the other ASEAN capitals) on the one hand, and Hanoi and Phnom Penh on the other, created a constant nightmare for UNICEF and ICRC, making them suspect to both sides precisely because they were compelled to work closely with both to carry out the relief program. To maintain credibility simultaneously on the border and in Phnom Penh, UNICEF/ICRC leadership evolved an extraordinary but highly effective diplomatic style, alternating condemnation with commendation on both fronts.

Every problem was seen in one capital or the other as an example of the intransigence or malicious intent of the "other side." One issue, for example, that poisoned the atmosphere was the claim emanating periodically from Western sources, apparently based on refugee debriefings at the border, that international food shipments were being diverted to Vietnam. These claims, although consistently denied by relief officials charged with monitoring distributions within the country, were a continuing cause of outrage to the Vietnamese, as well as a source of concern to the ASEAN group, who shared a generalized fear that the relief effort was strengthening the position of the Vietnamese. Similarly, the insistence of the Phnom Penh authorities on controlling food distribution, and their refusal to permit adequate international monitoring, convinced many Western officials that diversion was a deliberate policy.

Ultimately, it became clear to many U.S. officials, as had always been argued by the UN team, that bureaucratic obstacles in Phnom Penh were caused more by the incompetence of the raw and untrained government officials than by deliberate intent.

The fact that the Joint Mission was able to function so effectively under these circumstances testifies to the patience and persistence of the team in Phnom Penh, under John Saunders, and the energy and finesse of Sir Robert Jackson, the Secretary General's Special Coordinator for Kampuchean Relief, who managed to maintain necessary dialogue for the Joint Mission with Moscow as well as Hanoi.

History

Finally, in considering the circumstances surrounding the extraordinary international investment in aid to Kampuchea, we should not ignore the background of U.S. involvement in Indo-China and particularly the saturation bombing of what was then Cambodia. Not since the Civil War has there been a more divisive conflict in American history, and the most divisive episode of that war was the secret bombing of neutral Cambodia.

No one can measure the effects of this legacy with any certainty or gauge accurately its relative weight in the complex mix of political and strategic interests and humanitarian motives that moved the Carter administration and the Congress in their response to this crisis. But it is clear that without strong U.S. leadership, neither the Indochinese Resettlement Program nor the Kampuchean relief effort would have generated such extraordinary momentum. Both programs have contributed to the preservation of countless human lives and moderated an enormous quantum of human suffering. No one who witnessed the development of these initiatives at close range could fail to sense the impact of history on America's lead role.

III

What, then, is the lesson of this complicated experience in international relief? Of the "special factors" that helped to produce an extraordinary level of responses from the international community, all but one are virtually unique to Kampuchea. It seems unlikely that either geo-politics or history will weigh as heavily in the calculus of response among nations to future famine situations. But the capacity of the news media to inform the world, to bring home the reality of human suffering, and thereby to mobilize compassion, can make a decisive difference whenever the disaster of famine threatens. It may be that a group organized solely to sound the alert, so that the news media will focus on the situation sooner rather than later, could contribute substantially to the defeat of famine in future crises. Amnesty International and its work in aid of political prisoners suggests at least a partial model. Early warning alone, however, is not all that's needed. Something like Mrs. Carter's trip (or Liv Ullman's recent visit to Somalia) has to happen to activate the necessary private and public sector energies. Making that something happen must be a preoccupation for all of us from now on.

3

FEEDING CHINA'S ONE BILLION: PERSPECTIVES FROM HISTORY

Lillian M. Li

In April 1980 press reports revealed that in 1980 China suffered such serious damage from drought in the north and flooding in the middle Yangzi (Yangtze) valley that for the first time in thirty years it had to request international relief. It was estimated that 130 million people in nine provinces were "facing varying degrees of food shortages," and that 21 million had been "seriously affected."[1] This news came as a surprise not just to the general public but even to many China specialists because it has been widely thought that the People's Republic of China had substantially solved the problem of hunger, and that this had been its single greatest achievement.

In contrast to the China of the past where beggars were a familiar part of the landscape and where massive famines raged, it has been held that in China today everyone has enough to eat. This achievement has seemed all the more remarkable in view of the fact that, measured by almost any standard, China is still a very poor country, and its agricultural output over the past thirty years has barely kept pace with its rapid population growth from about 583 million in 1953 to close to one billion today.

In China, the elimination of hunger has been achieved not so much through economic growth and gains in productivity as through more equitable distribution of food and income. Through the grain-rationing system, everyone is presumably guaranteed a subsistence diet. Unlike many or most developing countries where income distribution is very skewed, the leveling of income in China, combined with the control of food distribution, has prevented gains in agricultural output from accruing only to those in the upper-income brackets. It is this system of distribution that has been the aspect of the "Maoist" model of development most admired abroad.

Today, however, many aspects of the "Maoist" model are being discredited within China itself. Official pronouncements have been increasingly frank in their revelations of the extent of past agricultural disasters and food short-

Lillian M. Li is an associate professor of history at Swarthmore College.

ages and in assigning blame to erroneous Maoist policies, especially those during the ten years of the Cultural Revolution, 1966–76. In Sichuan province, for example, between 1957 and 1976 the population grew from 72 to 95 million, but grain output increased from 23 to only 25 million metric tons.[2] This was said to have been the result of incompetent agricultural policy, which actually caused famine in 1976.[3] The most notable accomplishment of the present premier Zhao Ziyang was that he restored agricultural productivity to this area when he was head of the Sichuan Provincial Party Committee. An even more serious revelation, however, is that conditions in the aftermath of the Great Leap Forward, 1959–62, were in fact as devastating as critics outside China have claimed, and others have guessed. The economist Sun Yefang acknowledged recently that in 1960, the worst year, the death rate rose from 10.8 per thousand to 25.4 per thousand, implying 10 million excess deaths due to starvation.[4] Because of the overzealous policies of the Great Leap period, we know that total grain production dropped from 200 million metric tons in 1958 down to 150 million in 1960, and the 1958 level of production was not regained until 1964.[5]

Even if we say that such extraordinary subsistence crises were due to terrible human errors of the past which are not likely to be repeated, recent frank admissions by party leaders that a substantial portion of the Chinese population is undernourished are harder to dismiss. In 1979 former Vice-Premier Li Xiannian was reported to have said that 100 million Chinese were undernourished. Another often-cited statement in a Hong Kong source said that 200 million Chinese live on less than 300 *jin* (150 kg.) of food-grain ration a year.[6] Efforts outside China to estimate per capita food consumption on the basis of known production and population figures agree that the average per capita daily food consumption of Chinese is about 2,000 to 2,100 calories, and this represents no net gain over the best estimates for Chinese nutrition in the 1930s, when famine conditions were known to have been so grave.[7] According to Nicholas Lardy's latest study, the average Chinese annual per capita grain consumption in 1978 was only 196.5 kilograms which was 3.2 percent less than that for 1957.[8]

By standards of body weights and energy needs, an average of 2,100 calories a day should probably be sufficient,[9] but it leaves very little margin for waste or discretionary consumption. Moreover, the average Chinese diet is not only about as meager in caloric value as it was in the 1930s; it has not improved in its quality or variety either, being largely dependent on grains. About 90 percent of the caloric content of the Chinese diet is said to be from grains, and 80 percent of protein intake.[10] The average Chinese eats very little meat, although there has been a significant improvement in this area over the last few years. In 1977, average per capita meat consumption was 7.5 kilograms, but in 1980 it was up to 12 kilograms.[11] Staple products such as oil and sugar are also in short supply. Cooking oil is strictly rationed at 500 grams a month in Peking and below 300 grams in other areas. Sugar consumption is also very restricted.[12] Although urban residents report that food products, especially poultry and vegetables, are more readily attainable with the revival of free markets, there are still many bottlenecks and shortages for consumers, even in the most favorable urban environments.

If the system of food distribution were perfectly equitable, we might conclude that the average Chinese diet is adequate but rather uninteresting. However, it seems clear that a substantial sector of the population fails to receive this average diet, and that the distribution system is not perfectly equitable. There are two major sources of inequality, the first being regional. Although the evidence is partial, average per capita grain distribution—which is dependent on productivity—seems to vary greatly by province, with richer provinces such as Zhejiang receiving a significantly higher distribution than poor provinces such as Xinjiang.[13] The second major source of inequality is urban-rural. The urban population, conventionally said to be 20 percent of the total Chinese population, is acknowledged to have a higher grain ration than the rural population, according to one estimate at least 25 to 35 percent higher on the average.[14] Recently it has been shown that income levels within China are far more differentiated than previously thought, but income distribution in Chinese cities seems to be more equal than in cities in other developing societies, while income distribution in the countryside is less different from other developing societies.[15] In rural areas, it has been shown that even production teams within the same commune can differ significantly in their grain allotment and work-point values.[16]

Although China has thus far been able to regulate food consumption by guaranteeing a minimum standard of diet for the entire population, it now seems clear that limits of egalitarianism, and hence the prevention of hunger through the distribution system, have probably been reached. Over the next few years, the pressures on the distribution system can only increase. If the present economic policy continues, the use of material incentives in all economic enterprises, the expansion of the role of private plots, and the emphasis on the Four Modernizations (agriculture, industry, science and technology, and defense) may cause the distribution of income to become more uneven, and hence the demand for more and better food to increase. In the countryside the present movement to lower the unit of accounting from the production team to groups of households, single households, or even individuals, may produce the desired effect of increasing productivity, but this will almost certainly be at the cost of further skewing rural income distribution, which may well affect the level of food consumption.[17] In the cities, the drive to encourage intellectuals and technical personnel to improve their training and to assume a leading role in the modernization process can only lead to expectations of a higher level of consumption, which the state will not be able to ignore. The demand for better quality and more varied food will almost certainly include a greater demand for meat, which will place an additional pressure on the agricultural sector for feedgrain as well as foodgrain.[18]

Assuming that the current distribution system is about as equitable as can be achieved and is not likely to be improved upon, improvements in the food situation in China will be made only if gains in agricultural productivity exceed population increases. How likely is it that China can raise its agricultural productivity and at the same time keep its population growth down? Although Maoist policy toward population control was ambivalent or inconsistent in the 1950s and 1960s, during the 1970s there was a sustained birth control campaign, which has apparently been very successful in bringing down birth rates. John Aird, leading American authority on Chinese population, has recently written, "A demographic change that is without precedent in the human experience has apparently taken place within the last decade," but he also cautions, "From the limited information available, it is impossible to trace its course, identify its causes, or reach firm conclusions about its significance."[19] In any case, although no official figures for national vital rates have been released, foreign analysts generally believe that in 1977 China's birth rate was probably about 18 per thousand, its death rate 6.3 per thousand, yielding a 1.2 percent growth rate.[20] Even if this low growth rate is correct—and it is a remarkable achievement compared with the rest of Asia, matched only by Hong Kong and Singapore and bettered only by Japan—by the year 2000, China's population will still be well in excess of 1,200,000,000.

Between 1952 and 1977, grain production rose by 75 percent, at an average annual rate of 2.3 percent, barely keeping pace with an average annual 2.1 percent population growth.[21] China's current Ten-Year Plan calls for a growth rate of 3.5 percent per year in foodgrains, and a target of 400 million metric tons by 1985. Although most American analysts believe this target is too ambitious and cannot be met, they agree that a more modest target that will match China's short-term consumption needs can be met. The 1980 production was 318 million metric tons, down from 332 million in 1979. Bruce Stone estimates that an additional 63 million tons will be needed, which includes increased demand from population growth, direct distribution to lower income groups, increased livestock feeding, stockpiling, industrial use, food processing, and brewing.[22] In estimating future output, agricultural economists, however, disagree about the relative weight they wish to assign to technological and institutional factors. Some believe that better seed technology, increased use of chemical fertilizers, and expansion of irrigation can lead to continued modest improvement, but foresee serious technological and environmental constraints.[23] Others, however, believe that more efficient planning, particularly the current transition to price planning, as opposed to production planning, in and of itself will lead to an increase in productivity. The two major components of this new policy are (1) the use of comparative advantage in cropping decisions in different regions, which was not possible under the previous policy of regional grain self-sufficiency, and (2) the use of price incentives in planning.[24] Still others agree that better agricultural management will be the crucial determinant of future productivity, but are more cautious in their assessment of the magnitude of the results.[25]

In short, although China can rightly claim that it has succeeded in feeding its population, which has grown at an alarming rate over the past thirty years, it cannot, and the present leadership does not, claim to have "solved" the problem of hunger in China. Although most people seem to have a minimum subsistence, and the specter of large-scale famines has generally disappeared, nevertheless the margin in China is so thin that "man-made" crises such as the Great Leap Forward, or "natural" crises such as the recent drought and flood, could precipitate a disaster of sizeable proportions. For many foreigners, the news that China may not have found a permanent solution to its food problem may shatter some deeply held assumptions. Many Americans regard the People's Republic of China's ability to feed its population adequately as its greatest accomplishment, and some regard it as the sole reason for condoning a political system which they otherwise find distasteful. For some foreign critics, on the other hand, any sign of starvation or malnutrition in China is seen to be caused by the nature of the political system itself.[26]

This tendency to judge a political system on the basis of the success of its food policy is not, however, the unique creation of foreign China-watchers. It is, in fact, a reflection of the attitude of the Chinese themselves. Revelations about past agricultural disasters are being made by the present leadership in order to attack Maoist policies of the past, especially the policies of the "Gang of Four" during the years 1966–76. And before that, during the Great Leap Forward and its disastrous aftermath, it was Kuomintang propaganda from Taiwan that was the first to report starvation on the mainland, because it was regarded as *prima facie* evidence of the evils of the political enemy, and a sign of the failure of communism.

In fact, the attitude that natural disasters and political actions are intimately, and even causally, related has ancient Chinese roots that far antedate the twentieth-century political rivalries with which we are familiar. In the traditional Confucian political ideology, a dynasty was said to have received the "Mandate of Heaven" because it was morally fit to rule, but it would lose that mandate if it should lapse in its moral rule. In the downward swing of the so-called dynastic cycle, floods and droughts, together with rebellions, were taken as visible portents of the dynasty's impending loss of the Mandate of Heaven.

It is my view, however, that the "politicization" of the food question in China, both past and present, has been very much overdone. In the long historical view, it can readily be seen that there are certain fundamental problems with which all Chinese governments have had to contend, and that the range of possible solutions to these problems has perhaps been narrower than they, or we, would like to acknowledge. For the historian, in other words, there are certain continuities between the past and present which seem salient and which serve to put into perspective the role which the state can play in influencing the food/population problem.

The first thing to bear in mind is that China was not always a land of the starving masses, characterized by chronic suffering and periodic famines. Although there are records of famines dating back to ancient times, and although famines were recognized phenomena to be dealt with, the scale and frequency of famines in the nineteenth and twentieth centuries up to 1949 were probably unmatched by anything in the past, and may have been caused by extraordinary new factors: (1) population pressure, (2) internal disorder and dynastic decline, and (3) Western imperialist encroachment, the three being difficult to distinguish in their results. That conditions in modern China were more difficult than before will be hard for historians to prove definitively, but it may be well to emphasize the fact that China's population explosion did not occur until the eighteenth century, when its population apparently doubled from 150 million to over 300 million. The reasons for this eighteenth-century growth were various. It was a century of unprecedented internal prosperity and external expansion for the Chinese Empire. The Manchu dynasty encouraged the settlement of marginal or frontier lands by the population. In agriculture, two alternative, but not mutually exclusive, theories have been proposed: one that the population was able to expand because increasing traditional inputs of labor, irrigation, and better seeds permitted a substantial rise in rice yields, and the other that the introduction of new world crops—peanut, corn, and sweet potato—permitted the feeding of a larger population with nutritious crops which could be grown on poor soil.[27]

More recently, some colleagues of mine have been working on yet another type of explanation, namely, that the Chinese population could grow rapidly in the eighteenth century, even in the absence of a real agricultural revolution, i.e., a technological revolution, because the state possessed the institutional and financial means with which to counteract wide fluctuations in grain prices and to alleviate or prevent large-scale subsistence crises.[28] Although this is a daring and controversial idea which needs a great deal more historical research before it will be widely accepted, it is undeniable that the eighteenth-century Chinese state, which represented the traditional Chinese state in its strongest form, did possess remarkable instruments of influence and control, especially considering that the Chinese Empire extended for thousands of miles with only a primitive transporation network linking most places.

Among these were several tools by which the Chinese state could try to prevent or control famines. First, it had a bureaucracy which possessed a common Confucian educational background, which was selected by merit, and which served impartially all over China. One of the duties of the provincial governors was to present monthly reports on weather and grain prices to help monitor those conditions which might indicate an impending crisis. Governors were also supposed to contribute funds toward river conservancy in order to prevent flooding along major waterways. Secondly, there was a state granary system, which helped stabilize prices through sales and loans, and provided famine relief. During the eighteenth century it is estimated that these state granaries held about fifteen to twenty days' supply of grain on the average, not a bad record for a pre-modern state.[29] Thirdly, the government possessed a battery of techniques for famine relief. Although quite often the central government preferred to leave famine relief to local initiative, in case of large-scale crises in key areas, it could and did mobilize very effective

famine relief campaigns. In one case in 1743–44, studied by two of my colleagues, a potentially large-scale famine was averted when the government
moved into the drought-stricken area with emergency grain supplies, conducted house-to-house registration of famine victims, gave out emergency
relief, and opened up soup-kitchens. Because of the efficacy of such efforts,
one scholar has termed the eighteenth century "the golden age of famine
relief" in China.[30]

The actual effectiveness of Qing bureaucracy in famine prevention and
relief will continue to be a subject of study and debate among historians, and
no doubt some will continue to argue that many of the administrative
measures which we find described in the historical record were probably
never put into practice. The point I wish to make here is that the present
government of the People's Republic of China was not the first in China to
try to improve agricultural productivity and to avert crises, and moreover,
like it or not, it inherited a bureaucratic tradition. It has also inherited problems that are of very ancient origin and defy any permanent solutions. The
fundamental problems with which the PRC has had to contend are hardly
new and certainly not of its own creation. Here I will have time to discuss only
two broad problem areas.

The first area is that of regional differentiation, or put it another way,
interregional coordination. One of the most obvious things you can say about
China is that it is a very big country, but from that simple fact come many
profound and complex implications. China is a very big country, but its natural resources are very unevenly distributed. Only 11 percent of its land is
arable, and most of it is concentrated in the eastern half of the country, while
vast expanses of the northwest and southwest remain uncultivable. Moreover, even within the arable regions of China, there are wide disparities in
productivity due to different climatic conditions, soils, and water resources.
A traditional problem of the Chinese state was how to balance the resources
and interests of various regions. During the middle period of Chinese history,
for example, the politically powerful north was balanced against the
economically prosperous south. The shipment of grain tribute up the Grand
Canal from the lower Yangzi valley, the most productive agricultural section
of China, was a material expression of this trade-off, as the grain was largely
intended to feed the court at Beijing (Peking). By the eighteenth century, the
lower Yangzi valley itself became a grain-importing region because it had
shifted to a significant degree to the planting of cash crops. The bulk of the
grain deficit was made up by imports from the central Yangzi valley, a region
of rising agricultural productivity. While from an economic point of view this
was fundamentally a mutually beneficial exchange, from a political standpoint this growing interregional grain trade posed basic policy problems for
Qing officials. Local Hunan and Hubei people complained that in times of
poor harvest, the continuation of the grain export trade caused local prices to
reach a point where real hardship was felt, and they advocated the prohibi-
tion of exports.[31] Confucian political theory tended to favor the idea of local

agrarian self-sufficiency and had traditionally been hostile to mercantile activity and to merchants as a group, seeing them as basically unproductive, parasitic members of society. However, the statesmen of the eighteenth century were not unaware of the benefits of trade and comparative advantage, and we see throughout this period their very deep ambivalence on this question.

It might be said that this deep ambivalence has persisted to this very day. Although it has been a key policy of the Chinese government to encourage the settlement and development of border areas, it is nevertheless the case that enormous regional disparities still exist. In fact, agricultural productivity has grown least rapidly in these border areas, at the same time that their populations have experienced the highest rates of growth. During the period of the Cultural Revolution, regional self-sufficiency in grain became a major policy objective, and in some regions much land that had previously been planted in cash crops was converted to the growing of grain. The reckless pursuit of this policy has apparently led to some serious imbalances. At the present time the idea of regional grain self-sufficiency, as well as the goal of local self-sufficiency embodied in the Dazhai model, have both been rejected, and crop selection decisions are now being made along the lines of comparative advantage. To handle this, between 1977–78 and 1979–80, the state increased by 20 percent the amount of grain that it procured for redistribution to grain-deficit areas.[32] But it is clear that such policies may also tend in the long run to accentuate the wide difference in natural resources and other endowments of the different regions of China, and balancing their conflicting interests will continue to pose a major dilemma for the central government.

A second, and perhaps even more fundamental, problem area is that of environmental deterioration. It is well known that China has been burdened with several particularly intractable natural problems throughout the centuries. In the People's Republic of China, water control projects of mammoth proportions have been undertaken to try to bring China's rivers and other waterways under control. The building of large and small-scale dams, the cutting of diversionary canals to the ocean, and the continued building of dikes have all been undertaken on a most impressive scale and have done a great deal to bring the worst problems under some control. However, it is also clear that China's major environmental problems persist despite the attempts to alleviate them. The Yellow River, for example, has historically been China's single most dramatic natural problem. With a shallow bed running the course of over 3,000 miles, the Yellow River carries about 1.6 billion metric tons of silt each year, a quantity said to be seventeen times larger than the Nile and six times that of the Mississippi.[33] Over the centuries as it has run its course, the bed of the river has been built up so that it is now as many as ten meters higher than the surrounding countryside in some places and is retained only by very high dikes. When the summer rains are excessively heavy and these dikes break, as they have many times in China's history, the countryside, extremely flat at the North China Plain, becomes

flooded on a very large scale. A few times in the past century the Yellow River
has even shifted its route and caused extensive damage. Work on the Yellow
River has been impressive, but major problems persist, and the current press
still contains discussions and proposals for a "permanent" solution.[34]

The recent drought in north China is also the repetition of a familiar historical pattern. Although it was described as the worst drought in thirty-eight
years, north China is, however, subject to frequent droughts, as the rainfall is
concentrated almost entirely in the three summer months. Although many
tube-wells have been sunk along the north China plain, and other irrigation
measures have been taken in the past thirty years, a recent Chinese press
report admits that the problems of drought, waterlogging, alkalinity, and
salinity still persist, and yields are much lower than the national average.[35]
The flood of the Yangzi River in Hubei, although the worst in 26 years according to press reports, is also part of a familiar historical pattern. In this
area the likelihood of flooding has over the past few centuries been greatly
exacerbated by a continual process of land reclamation, which started in the
fourteenth century, and which by the nineteenth century had made a virtual
internal delta of this area.[36] Reclamation and intensive cultivation of this rich
land made possible the interregional grain trade mentioned earlier, but it also
made the area more vulnerable to flooding. Although in the PRC much attention has been paid to control of the Yangzi, what is surprising is not that
there was such a flood in 1980 but that it did not happen earlier.

The pressure of population on the land was responsible for this drive to
reclaim land, and it continues unabated today. For every such effort, however, it seems that an ecological price has to be paid. The drive toward regional grain self-sufficiency, for example, has prompted the conversion of
grasslands in the border areas of China—Inner Mongolia, Ningxia, Gansu,
Xinjiang, and Tibet—and this has resulted in destroying the balance of the
ecosystem. Soil erosion and desertification have taken place at an alarming
rate.[37] Deforestation, another serious aspect of environmental deterioration,
is also a centuries-old problem. Although massive campaigns for reforesta-
tion have taken place, at the same time the loss of forestland through legal
and illegal means is taking place at a disturbing rate.[38]

Historians, of course, are professionally predisposed to see the continuities
in the course of human events. By no means do I wish to leave you with the
impression that I think nothing has changed in China for the past two or three
hundred years. On the contrary, the China of today is strikingly different
from the China of 1800, 1900, or even 1949. For one thing, there are more
than three times the number of people in China today than there were in the
year 1800. For another, the problem of environmental deterioration is potentially more serious now than it was then. At the same time, however, the
technological resources available to deal with agriculture and the environment are also much greater. All I have meant to suggest in this talk is that in
dealing with the challenge of feeding a billion people in a large, complex

country of many regions and in an environment with many dangers, the Chinese government today faces a problem of such large dimensions that politics, policy, and human will alone cannot be expected to account for everything or take care of all problems. Does this mean that politics does not count, or that policy does not matter? On the contrary, it puts a greater premium than ever on policy, as there is a narrower margin for human error, but at the same time the limits of human and political action must always be kept in perspective.

NOTES

1. *New York Times,* April 25, 1981.
2. Nicholas R. Lardy, "Food Consumption in the People's Republic of China," draft chapter for Randolph Barker and Radna Sinha, eds., *The Chinese Agricultural Economy* (Boulder: Westview Press, forthcoming), p. 9.
3. Vice-premier Deng Xiaoping admitted this in an interview with Han Suyin in 1977, cited in Vaclav Smil, "China's Food: Availability, Requirements, Composition, and Prospects," *Food Policy* 6 (May 1981): 71.
4. Sun Yefang, "Jiaqiang tongji gongzuo, gaige tongji tizhi," *Jingji guanli* 2 (Feb. 15,1981): 3-5, trans. in Foreign Broadcast Information Service 81-058, March 26, 1981.
5. Anthony M. Tang, "Food and Agriculture in China: Trends and Projections, 1952-77 and 2000," in Anthony M. Tang and Bruce Stone, *Food Production in the People's Republic of China,* International Food Policy Research Institute, Research Report 15 (May 1980), p. 26. According to Nicholas Lardy, "Planning and Productivity in Chinese Agriculture," unpublished paper (August 1980), p. 12, the 1957 output was not regained until 1966.
6. Lardy, "Food Consumption," p. 2, and Smil, "China's Food," p.72, cite various statements to this effect.
7. Several recent studies have come to the same general conclusion although they have employed different methods. See Lardy, "Food Consumption," pp. 4-4a and Smil, "China's Food," p. 70. See also Thomas Wiens, "Agricultural Statistics in the People's Republic of China," in Alexander Eckstein, ed., *Quantitative Measurements of China's Economic Output* (Ann Arbor: University of Michigan Press, 1980), pp. 67-78, 97-99.
8. Lardy, "Food Consumption," pp. 12-12b. This calculation is based on processed or fine grains; also Smil, "China's Food," p. 72.
9. Smil, "China's Food," p. 70.
10. Ibid., p. 69.
11. U.S. Department of Agriculture, *Agricultural Situation: People's Republic of China, Review of 1980, and Outlook for 1981* (Washington, D.C., 1981), p. 11.
12. Smil, "China's Food," p. 74.
13. Bruce Stone, "China's 1985 Foodgrain Production Target: Issues and Aspects," in Tang and Stone, *Food Production,* p. 95; and Lardy, "Food Consumption," p. 12a.
14. Lardy, "Food Consumption," p. 12b, and correspondence with the author, May 21, 1981.
15. William L. Parish, "Egalitarianism in Chinese Society," *Problems of Communism* 30 (Jan.-Feb. 1981): 39-42.
16. William L. Parish and Martin King Whyte, *Village and Family in Contemporary China* (Chicago: University of Chicago Press, 1978), pp. 54-59.
17. A recent article in *Beijing Review,* January 19, 1981, entitled "Let Some Localities and Peasants Prosper First," addresses this problem, but denies that it will be serious. At the same time, however, it points out that the state has set up a development fund to aid poor brigades, teams, and peasants who have fallen behind.
18. The consequences of this change in diet, and China's larger role in the international grain market, especially the corn market, are analyzed by C. Peter Timmer, "China and the World Food System" (unpublished paper, 1981).
19. John S. Aird, "Fertility Decline in China," in Nick Eberstadt, ed., *Fertility Decline in the Less Developed Countries* (New York: Praeger, 1981), p. 193.

20. Ibid., p. 140.

21. Tang, "Food and Agriculture in China," p. 13.

22. Stone, "China's 1985 Food Production Target," p. 86.

23. This is generally the view of Randolph Barker, Daniel Sisler, and Elizabeth Rose, "Prospects for Growth in Grain Production," in Barker and Sinha, *The Chinese Agricultural Economy.*

24. This is the basic thesis of Nicholas Lardy, in his "Planning and Productivity in Chinese Agriculture."

25. Thomas B. Wiens, "The Evolution of Policy and Capabilities in China's Agricultural Technology," in *The Chinese Economy Post-Mao* (Washington, D.C.: Joint Economic Committee of the Congress of the United States, 1978), p. 703.

26. For example, Miriam London and Ivan D. London, "Hunger in China: The Failure of a System?" *Worldview* 22: 10 (October 1979): 44–49.

27. These are the views of Dwight H. Perkins, *Agricultural Development in China, 1368–1968* (Chicago: Aldine, 1969), and Ping-ti Ho, *Studies on the Population of China, 1368–1953* (Cambridge: Harvard University Press, 1959), respectively.

28. This was an idea discussed at the Workshop on Food and Famine in Chinese History, held at Harvard University in August 1980. Several members of the workshop are preparing a handbook on grain supply and granaries in China during the Qing period.

29. Ts'ui-jung Liu, "A Reappraisal of the Granary System during Ch'ing China (1644–1911)," in *Academia Economic Papers* 8: 1 (March 1980):1–31 (in Chinese).

30. Pierre-Etienne Will, *Bureaucratie et famine en Chine au 18ᵉ siècle* (Paris: Mouton, 1980). Roy S. Y. Yim is also working on the 1743–44 crisis in his dissertation for Oxford University.

31. R. Bin Wong, "Food Distribution Crises: Markets, Granaries and Food Riots in the Qing Period," unpublished paper for the Workshop on Food and Famine in Chinese History (1980).

32. Lardy, "Planning and Productivity," p. 58.

33. Vaclav Smil, "Controlling the Yellow River," *The Geographical Review* 69: 3 (July 1979): 256.

34. See, for example, *Renmin Ribao* (The People's Daily), January 15, 1981, in Joint Publications Research Service, 77577, March 12, 1981.

35. *Guangming Ribao,* August 7, 1980, in Joint Publications Research Service, 76802, November 12, 1980.

36. This process is documented by Pierre-Etienne Will, "Un Cycle hydraulique en Chine: La province du Hubei du XVIᵉ au XIXᵉ siècles," *Bulletin de l'Ecole Française* 68 (1980): 261–287.

37. Lardy, "Planning and Productivity," pp. 21–22, and Vaclav Smil, "Environmental Degradation in China," *Asian Survey* 20: 8 (August 1980): 783–784.

38. Smil, "Environmental Degradation," pp. 785–787. An article in the People's Daily decries the illegal cutting of trees in Hubei province in 1980. See *Renmin Ribao,* January 17, 1981, in Joint Publications Research Service, 77642, March 23, 1981.

4

THE CLINICAL FACE OF FAMINE IN SOMALIA

Kevin M. Cahill, M.D.

Famine is no stranger on the Horn of Africa. Prolonged periods of drought and hunger are as integral a part of the life of the Somali nomad as April showers and apple pie are for Americans. Seasons of semi-starvation in Somalia have become the legends of a hardy race; poems recall the pangs of hunger, the relative joys of brackish water, and the confidence that, in crises, true friends help.

The great Somali poet, Mohamed Abdile Hassan, described drought on the Horn:

> Charred plants, stumps of burned trees,
> the hot air rising from them,
> The burnt branches and tree trunks
> through which you pass in pain.

In the midst of famine he further noted:

Who welcomes you like a kinsman in your day of need
and who, at the height of the drought, does not bar his gate against you,
Is not he who never fails you in your weakness one of the brethren?

During the past twenty years I have studied the health problems of Somalia and shared in the clinical care of refugees there during two major periods of famine—at the end of the Sahelian drought in 1976 and, in the past few years, during the ongoing Ogaden conflict.[1]

Somalia is now home to the *largest refugee population in the world*, with over 1,300,000 persons in makeshift camps, and some 3,000 new victims arriving every day.[2] The present calamity had its origins in what a United Nations report euphemistically terms the "troubles in the Horn of Africa." The "troubles" include the bombing and strafing by Russian and Cuban pilots of

Kevin M. Cahill, M.D., is the director of the Tropical Disease Center, Lenox Hill Hospital, New York City.

nomads who have, from time immemorial, trekked with their camels from well to well across the barren Horn searching for water. Geographic boundaries mean nothing to nomads, for their life is basically a constant circuit along a series of wells, rejoicing with the very occasional rains, nourishing their cattle and, in good years, being able to sell some of their herds for export to the Arabian Peninsula.

Somalia is one of the least developed countries in the world; total annual per capita income is less that $175. They are, however, an enormously proud people and the philosophy of the present government, in power since 1969, is one of self-reliance. Therefore, when the first refugees began to flow over the political boundaries of Somalia, they were received as brothers and sisters, and absorbed into the rural population of Somalia. Despite the wrenching poverty of Somalia, that government asked for no official help from anyone.

As opposed to the obscene spectacle in Southeast Asia, where refugees have been forced back to sea from the shores of "host" countries, or shot at the borders, or forced to return to certain death—refugees in Somalia were welcomed to share the meager food and shelter of their fellow nomads. Soon, however, the general population could no longer absorb refugees. Camps were then set up and there are currently twenty-six large refugee camps in Somalia, with multiple small transient stations at the border. To reach the transient camps many of the refugees I met had traveled thirty to forty days, moving only at night, for they would be strafed during the day. I personally examined patients with bloody, shattered limbs and gangrenous wounds who had been carted on the backs of camels for weeks.

The most striking feature about the refugees in Somalia today is that over 90 percent of them are women and children; the men have either been killed or have remained in the Ogaden to fight with the Western Liberation Movement. Thus the refugees are not only the most vulnerable in society, but they arrive in vast numbers, frail, malnourished, ill and, as noted, in many cases wounded. The number of Somali refugees in camps grows relentlessly.

In the best of times the medical services of Somalia are minimal, food is frequently scarce, safe water and adequate sanitation are almost nonexistent. When one imposes a million and a half additional people on that fragile structure, the potential for overwhelming infectious disease epidemics is almost certain. Within the refugee camps such epidemics are already a reality.

Mortality rates in Somalia are among the highest in the world. Now added to that already unstable health base are refugee camps averaging forty to fifty thousand people per camp. There is no safe drinking water. I did not see a single sanitary structure, or even a simple latrine. The nutritional level varies from poor to terrible, and some 25 percent of the young children and women are clearly in the throes of starving to death. The U.S. Center for D sease Control (CDC) has documented levels of malnutrition in Somalia *greater than any previously recorded*; some 37 percent of the children in one camp showed clinical evidence of severe protein malnutrition.

A brief survey by the World Health Organization team showed that 60 percent of the children in camps have glandular enlargement, with the primary cause being tuberculosis. In one camp that I visited, with 45,000 people, there had been forty-one deaths among pregnant women in the week that I was there; all deaths were due to infectious diseases. To put that in perspective I would like to note that there were twenty-eight deaths in all the pregnant women in New York State in 1980; only one fatality was due to infection, and that from a self-induced abortion. There had been 2,000 deaths in that camp in the preceding two weeks. There was one doctor to cope with this staggering situation. There was no immunization service in the camps for the simple reason that there were no vaccines. In fact, there are almost no medications of any kind available.

So that we not lose sight of the searing fact that the economic, social, political, and even ethical facets of famine all derive their significance from the suffering of individual human beings I present in this chapter the common physical signs of famine. Those people most severely affected—usually the young and the very old—present a clinical picture of great variety. At one end of the spectrum are the walking ghosts with marasmus, the victims of rapid, extensive caloric deficiency or, in a single word, starvation. At the opposite end are those suffering from chronic protein deficiency, or kwashiorkor. As in most disease states, the majority fall between these classic poles; the clinical picture is further complicated by almost universal infection with multiple parasites.

MARASMUS

The child with marasmus leaves the impression of an old man's face on an infant's body. There is obvious wasting of muscles with total loss of subcutaneous fat. The buttocks disappear and the skin is loose and wrinkled. Scrawny limbs seem incapable of supporting the typical swollen body. The bony skull appears disproportionately large, and the knees stand out as awkward knobs. Eye lesions are common and skin rashes, with infected "tropical ulcers," are almost universal. Diarrhea is the rule and complete rectal prolapse from weakness of the anal orifice is not uncommon. A simple measurement of the height and weight on a growth chart will document marked stunting. Nevertheless, the marasmic child is almost surprisingly alert, showing constant indications of hunger such as sucking and grasping movements. They are, however, patently weak and rapidly tire, becoming short of breath after the slightest exertion.

This clinical picture is not due solely to starvation but reflects the added burden of multiple parasitic infestations and respiratory infections. Malaria is extremely common and measles and tuberculosis are rife.

KWASHIORKOR

This is the other major protein deficiency disease in Somalia. It was almost unknown to the nomads because their customary diet of camel's milk and occasional goat meat is very rich in protein. I cannot recall seeing a single case of kwashiorkor in Somalia before the Sahelian drought of 1976, and there is surely nothing subtle about the striking features of kwashiorkor in the black African.

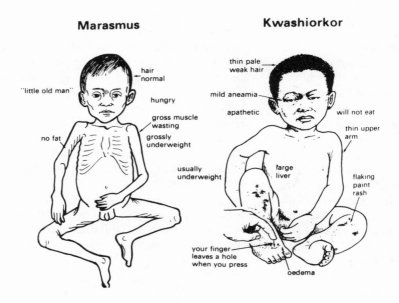

The hair turns a soft red or white and becomes straight and limp. The moon faces and swollen bodies have not the texture of a healthy cherubic child, but rather are pitted with edematous fluid. These children are apathetic or constantly whining. Skin rashes range from a dry, scaly, dark, "crazy pavement" pattern to almost total desquamation and severe ulcerations. The skin is often cold, and many children die of hypothermia when they are moved from the warmth of the mother's body. Obvious heart failure and ocular signs of vitamin A deficiency complete the clinical picture.

There are no laboratories in Somali refugee camps. Fortunately, there is little need for scientific confirmation to permit a working diagnosis for either marasmus or kwashiorkor. Therapy can be extremely challenging and deaths can be caused by inappropriate actions as well as neglect. Forced feeding can precipitate both diarrhea and aspiration pneumonia. Washing a child can exacerbate hypothermia, and it is better to have a dirty child than a dead one. The careful replacement of fluids, calories, and specific nutrients must be coordinated with the therapy for concurrent infections.

Even in optimal circumstances—which hardly describe a Somali refugee camp—the period of rehabilitation for a patient with marasmus is judged in terms of months, rather than days, and the pressure of new problems for an overworked health team frequently results in inadequate attention during recovery, inevitably ending in rapid deterioration and death.

The role of a physician in managing a catastrophic famine is not limited to the traditional diagnostic and therapeutic approach to the profession. He or she must learn to organize truck convoys, establish basic camps, and develop a team that will enable the foods donated or purchased to reach the hungry masses. The physician-leader, in this situation, must emphasize hope rather than disease, offering a future to those who have lost their past.

Medical school training rarely prepares one for such challenges. The essential qualities required to effectively serve in such situations are not built on technical details that can be memorized but must be based rather on the broad traditions that once made medicine a learned profession.

The clinical faces of famine in Somalia are seared in my mind. The photograph facing the Epilogue of this book tells a tale that few can evade, for it stares into our souls.

NOTES

1. Kevin M. Cahill, *Health on the Horn of Africa* (London: Spottiswoode, 1959); "Studies in Somalia," *Transactions of the Royal Society of Tropical Medicine* 65 (1970): 30; *Somalia; A Perspective* (Albany: SUNY Press, 1980); *New York Times*, Op Ed, July 18, 1977; New York *Daily News*, Op Ed, April 23, 1981.

2. New York *Daily News*, Op Ed, December 4, 1979.

5

DEMOGRAPHIC RESPONSES TO FAMINE

John Bongaarts
Mead Cain

In considering the demographic effects of famine it is necessary to make a distinction between short- and long-term responses. The former are primarily mediated through biological processes, while the latter involve behavioral adjustments to the crisis. In the presentation that follows, these two perspectives are treated separately.

THE SHORT-TERM RESPONSE

The disruption of the normal functions of society and the physiological stress on individuals during famines (defined by widespread starvation and heavy excess mortality) invariably result in large changes in the basic demographic processes. Measures of mortality, fertility, and population growth all undergo major deviations from the levels prevailing before the onset of the famine. Often the same can be said about migration behavior. The discussion of these phenomena is complicated by the fact that demographic responses vary widely, depending on the nature of the famine, and it is therefore not possible to describe a unique standard pattern of demographic change. Instead an attempt will be made here to extract from the records of a number of famines the main features that are found fairly consistently, while ignoring secondary and more variable aspects. To facilitate the presentation of the findings, the discussion will be illustrated with an example of hypothetical, but not atypical, demographic responses which can be expected during and immediately following a moderately severe famine of approximately a half year's duration with a well demarcated beginning and end. This hypothetical pattern attempts to model the famine experiences of contemporary developing countries, such as Bangladesh, which are demographically characterized by high levels of fertility and rapid rates of population growth.

Dr. John Bongaarts and Dr. Mead Cain are members of the Population Council.

Mortality

A rise in mortality is likely to be the most immediate and visible demographic consequence of famine. The simplest measure of the severity of a famine is the number of excess deaths, i.e., the number of deaths over and above those that would have occurred if previous nutritional conditions had prevailed. In some of the largest recent famines for which estimates exist, the number of excess deaths runs into the millions: around 2 million during the great Bengal famine of 1943 and about 1.5 million deaths in Bangladesh in 1974–1975.[1]

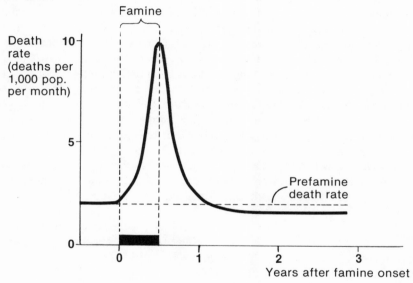

Figure 1. Death rate response to famine

The overall pattern of the death rate during and following a famine is outlined in Figure 1. Three distinct phases can be distinguished. First, during the famine period itself the death rate rises, slowly in the first weeks and then more rapidly as reserves are depleted and resistance to disease declines. Maximum mortality is observed at the end of the famine, when the death rate can reach levels several times higher than usual. Second, during the post famine period mortality will not immediately return to prefamine levels for some time, even if, as is done here, one assumes that food availability returns quickly to previous levels. The weakened physiological condition of most people will allow disease to take a substantial further toll in human lives. Finally, a year or more after the famine the death rate can fall significantly below the prefamine level and remain lower for several years because the least vulnerable subgroups in the population have the highest probability of surviving. (For simplicity, seasonal variations around the prefamine levels are ignored in the illustrations.)

The impact of famine mortality is usually distributed very unequally among different economic and demographic groups in the society. The landless and the poor will be the most affected. For example, in Bangladesh in 1974, households with less than 2.5 acres of land experienced a death rate three times higher than did households with more than 2.5 acres.[2] Several high-risk demographic subgroups can also be identified:

Infants. The year following birth is normally one associated with high mortality in poor developing countries (15 to 20 percent dying in the first year is not unusual). During a famine infant mortality rises further as diseases become more widespread, as birth weights decline, and as protein calorie malnutrition increases. Fortunately, this highly vulnerable age group can and often is protected from extreme mortality if breast milk, the infant's ideal form of nutrition, is provided. The rise in mortality among breastfeeding infants is therefore much less than that among older children.[3]

Children. This is the age group that is hardest hit by famine.[4] During the years up to puberty the body requires a substantial and well-balanced diet for optimal growth. Low calorie and protein intake stunts growth and allows disease to take its toll. The age group from one to three years, following weaning from breast milk, is especially at risk.

The Elderly. Mortality among the elderly rises sharply, but the overall effect on the death rate is relatively small because the aged make up only a small proportion of the total population in a typical developing country (e.g., about 5 percent of the total is over age sixty).

Pregnant and Lactating Women. The heavy additional nutritional demands made on the woman's body during pregnancy and breastfeeding are extremely difficult to meet during periods of food shortages. As a consequence, there is a sharp drop in the average birth weight of babies born during famines and breastfeeding and pregnant women become rapidly emaciated. However, breastfeeding can and does continue during the early phases of famines as long as adequate nipple stimulation to the breast is maintained by the suckling infant. This greatly benefits the infant, but puts a heavy strain on the mother.

It is difficult to make generalizations about the specific causes of famine mortality, partly because they vary with the nature of the famine, the health and nutritional status of the population before the onset of starvation, the extent of relief efforts and other factors, and partly because available evidence is inadequate. It should be noted, however, that starvation per se is often not the main cause of death. Instead, there is a large increase in mortality from endemic infectious diseases to which the nutritionally deprived population has greatly reduced resistance.

Following the famine-related surge in mortality, the death rate has a tendency to fall below previously prevailing levels. This is the result of a selection for the healthiest, strongest, and economically most advantaged individuals among the survivors. A severe famine produces a substantially altered population age composition, with more individuals in the central age groups and fewer in the oldest and youngest age groups. Since mortality risks are relatively low in the central age groups, the death rate will be reduced. This effect on the death rate can continue to be felt for many years but it only partially offsets the excess mortality of the famine.

Fertility

Although somewhat smaller in magnitude than the variations in the death rate, the famine-induced changes in the birth rate are substantial in the short term. Figure 2 presents the birth rate's fairly complex response pattern. During the famine itself, fertility remains virtually stable. This indicates that pregnancies already established at the start of the famine are well protected and are not at significantly increased risk of premature termination. Apparently, the nutritional and other physiological requirements of the fetus can be met by drawing on the mother's reserves and spontaneous intrauterine mortality is only marginally affected. This is especially true during the early months of gestation when the fetus is small. Toward the end of the pregnancy, the fetus becomes more susceptible to the general health and nutritional status of the mother, and as a consequence the birth weights of newborns decline substantially.[5] The stillbirth rate increases, but even a large proportional increase in this rate has little absolute impact on fertility because only a few percent of all births are stillborn.

The principal fertility response occurs nine months following the famine

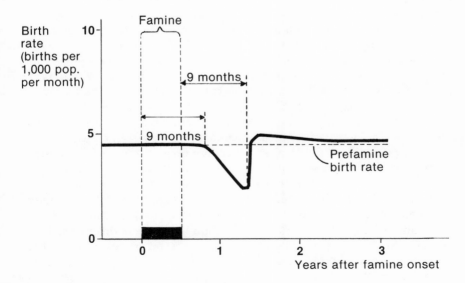

Figure 2. Birth rate response to famine

period. The birth rate declines and the extent of the decline is directly proportional to the severity of the famine. For example, in Matlab Thana, an area in Bangladesh markedly affected by the 1974 famine, the birth rate dropped by about a third.[6] After the Dutch famine from October 1944 to April 1945 the birth rate was cut by more than half,[7] and in Leningrad, where the starvation was even more severe and prolonged, infertility became virtually total.[8]

The timing of the delayed response clearly indicates that the fertility decline is caused by a reduction in the rate of conception during the famine. Several factors have been identified as contributing to this deficit in conceptions:[9]

—A decrease in fecundity (i.e., the biological capacity to reproduce). As starvation progresses, substantial proportions of women stop menstruating and ovulating and, in the male, sperm mobility and longevity are reduced. Amenorrhea and anovulation is partly caused by malnutrition and partly by the psychological stresses associated with the crisis.

—A lower frequency of intercourse. This is a result of a decline in libido, the general physical weakening of adults in the reproductive age groups, and a separation of spouses owing to temporary migration of the male in search of food or work.

—An increase in voluntary birth control efforts through contraception, abstention, or induced abortion.

—Postponement of new marriages.

With the restoration of food provisions to prefamine levels, the conception rate recovers quickly. There is no apparent lasting damage to the population's ability to reproduce.[10] In fact, the interval of depressed fertility is followed by one of excess fertility (see Figure 2). This phenomenon is not (or only to a very minor extent) due to a deliberate change in fertility behavior or to a desire for more births in developing countries in which fertility is close to its natural level. In these populations, little or no contraception is practiced so that fertility cannot be raised by removing such deliberate constraints. Instead, the explanation for the excess fertility is found in the biology of the reproductive process. Detailed studies of the childbearing process in developing countries with high fertility have revealed that women are not at risk of conceiving for large parts of their potential reproductive years either because they are pregnant or because they experience periods of temporary postpartum anovulation during breastfeeding. In a typical case, one may find that only about one in four women is actually in the ovulatory state and at risk of conceiving. The famine disturbs this normal distribution of women among different reproductive states. The decline in the conception rate and the rise in infant mortality during the famine cause a reduction in the proportion of women that are pregnant or anovulatory due to breastfeeding. The corresponding rise in the proportion of women in the exposed ovulatory state then produces an excess level of conceptions immediately following the famine and this in turn yields the fertility surplus nine months later. The birth rate may exceed the pre-famine level for up to three years,[11] but the excess fertility only partly compensates for the preceding deficit.

Migration

Compared with the other demographic variables, the migration response to famine is much less predictable and more dependent on particular circumstances. A detailed discussion of this complex subject is beyond the scope of this essay and only a brief comment will be made here.

Generally one observes substantial out-migration from the stricken area during the famine, followed by return migration in the months afterwards. The magnitude of out-migration varies directly with the availability of food in nearby areas (e.g., towns, cities, unaffected rural areas, and sometimes neighboring countries), with the distance to these relief centers, and with the availability of means of transportation. If large geographic areas are affected by the famine and few relief centers are within reach of the starving population, then migration may be a relatively small component of overall population change. On the other hand, if the starving population is given the opportunity to escape, massive migration can result. The exodus to the United States and other countries from Ireland during and after the famine in the 1840s is an extreme example, where the total number of out-migrants exceeded the number of deaths attributable to starvation.[12]

The extent of in-migration after the crisis depends on the prospects for a return of normal economic conditions. If the famine is caused by an unusual crop failure and the future potential for agricultural production is not impaired, then most out-migrants may be expected to return. However, in cases where a prolonged drought has affected the ability of the land to support the population, as for example in the Sahel region, out-migration is likely to be more permanent.

Interaction among demographic variables

Up to this point in the discussion, the processes of fertility, mortality, and migration have been considered to operate independently from one another. This is an acceptable abstraction of reality if one is interested in the principal features of the demographic response to famine, but there are also a number of interaction effects. These should be mentioned briefly, because they provide additional insights and they may explain unexpected findings in special cases.

—Mortality-fertility: High mortality in the youngest and oldest age groups produces an age composition with an unusually high concentration of adults in the reproductive years. This inflates some measures of fertility, in particular the crude birth rate, which then becomes an unreliable indicator of the actual level of fertility.

—Fertility-morality: The sharp drop in the birth rate is necessarily followed by a deficit of infants and young children. The reduction of the size of these age groups, which are subject to relatively high mortality risks, yields a lower death rate after the famine than would have been observed without the decline in fertility.

—Migration-mortality: The large scale movement of people facilitates the spread of infectious diseases. In addition, the stress of moving over long distances, often by walking, contributes to higher mortality. On the other hand, excess mortality in the stricken area may be somewhat reduced by migration as fewer people compete for the limited amounts of available food.

—Fertility-migration: The reduction in conceptions leaves fewer women in the pregnant and lactation phases of the reproductive cycle. The removal of these added nutritional burdens makes migration somewhat less difficult than it would have been otherwise.

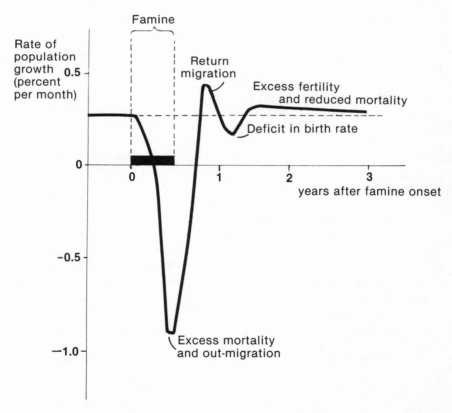

Figure 3. Response of the population growth rate to famine.

The population growth rate

Having examined each of the vital processes, we can now turn to their combined effect on the rate of population growth. With the basic demographic balancing equation, the rate of population growth is calculated as the birth rate minus the death rate plus the difference of out- and in-migration rates. Figure 3 summarizes the fluctuations in the growth rate during and following a famine in a geographic area heavily affected by starvation. It is assumed that the birth and death rate patterns given in Figures 1 and 2 prevail and that the majority of out-migrants from the area return after the crisis (this migration component is the least predictable demographic component). The population growth rate oscillates around the prefamine level, starting with a steep drop during the famine itself. For a brief interval the growth rate turns sharply negative due to excess mortality and out-migration. Shortly following the crisis the growth rate rises to above normal levels, as migrants return and mortality declines, but growth declines again to low levels when the deficit in the birth rate takes effect. In the final phase of the response, a slightly elevated growth rate is observed that is due to both excess fertility and lowered mortality. It should be emphasized that the assumptions on which Figure 3 are based were chosen so as to bring out clearly the major demographic forces operating to modify the growth rate. In reality, one may see a more blurred picture especially if the famine should last longer than half a year and if it is followed by a period of social and economic instability. In that case, the population growth rate may remain negative for a year or longer because the slower mortality decline and the lower pace of return migration can overlap with the dip in the birth rate.

The population size

What, finally, is the famine's impact on the size of population of the affected geographic area? Needless to say, the effect depends on a wide variety of circumstances, most of which have already been mentioned. We will briefly comment on the contribution made by each of the demographic processes:

—Fertility: The fluctuations in the birth rate have on the whole the least effect on the population size, partly because the deviations from the normal levels are smaller than the changes in the death rate and partly because the birth rate deficit is compensated by a period of excess births.

—Migration: As was discussed earlier, the impact of this component varies from very large (as in the Irish famine) to minimal, depending on the population's ability to migrate out of the stricken areas during the famine and on the extent of the return migration afterwards.

—Mortality: A large rise in the death rate is a consistent feature of all famines. Millions of deaths occurred during recent famines, causing a drop in the size of the population. Somewhat surprisingly, however, it can be demonstrated that these large numbers of deaths have only a modest effect on the population size. Take, for example, the Bangladesh famine of 1974. If one accepts Alamgir's estimate of 1.5 million excess deaths (and some observers believe this estimate to be too high), then "only" 2 percent of the total 1974 population of Bangladesh (74 million) died as a consequence of the famine. Since the average annual growth rate of Bangladesh is nearly 3 percent, the excess deaths are made up in less than one year.

The principal conclusion from this overview of short-term demographic responses to major recent famines is clear: changes in mortality and fertility have provided little in the way of a check on longer-term trends in overall size of the affected population. While the increase in the death rate and the reduction in the birth rate do limit the population growth rate for a brief period, this deficit is quickly made up as normal population growth rates—ranging from two to four percent per year in much of the developing world—resume. The famine's population impact is further limited by a compensatory excess in the birth rate and a deficit in the death rate for some years following the famine. On the other hand, out-migration can cause major and permanent reductions in the population of the famine-stricken areas.

THE LONG-TERM BEHAVIORAL RESPONSE

The preceding section described the immediate response to famine—a surge in mortality, decline in the rate of conception followed by a depression in the fertility rate, subsequent recovery of the death rate aided by a process of selection, and a compensatory surge in fertility. With the exception of migration, this pattern of short-term response can also be viewed as biological rather than behavioral. In the remainder of this essay we focus on the long-term demographic response to famine and its potentially serious consequences for future economic and social development.

Modern famine-prone societies share a number of common features. They are, without exception, located in the developing areas of the world. They are poor, with large portions of their populations living close to the margin of subsistence in "normal" years. It is the combination of low per capita and highly skewed distributions of wealth and income that make famine a real threat to these societies. In addition these societies are dominantly agrarian and they are subject to wide potential fluctuations in the yield or price of domestic food-grain crops—yields because of natural disasters and a variety of factors, including the vagaries of the international economy. Almost by definition, governments of famine-prone areas are either unable or unwilling to respond to crises in a timely and effective fashion. If adequate public relief measures were always taken, there would obviously be no famine.

An additional feature that areas currently exposed to the threat of famine have in common is rapid population growth. It seems evident that the persistence of high fertility and rapid population growth in regions such as South Asia can only increase the probability of famines occurring in the future. Over the decade of the 1970s, for example, the rate of population growth in Bangladesh exceeded the growth rate of domestic food production by a considerable margin.[13] The food-grain requirements that this rapidly growing population define have come to dominate public policy and public resources in a way that undermines the government's capacity to prevent famine in the event of future crisis, or to plan for positive economic development.

What are the prospects for abatement of the rapid population growth currently experienced by the developing countries? The historical pattern of demographic transition in the industrial West would suggest that current high rates of fertility will eventually decline to a level that approximates already low mortality rates, and in this way demographic equilibrium will be regained. But the situation of the developing countries of today is unprecedented in several respects, and thus the historical experience of the West may prove to be a poor guide. The current situation is unprecedented because of the rapidity of mortality decline and the extraordinarily high rates of growth that have resulted. Mortality declined at a more gradual pace in the West and population growth never approached the rates that have been typical of developing countries in the past few decades. More importantly, however, modern mortality decline has occurred without the structural change and economic development that accompanied mortality decline and demographic transition in the West. This latter characteristic leaves the future course of fertility in developing countries very much in doubt.

One can no longer simply assume that current high rates of fertility will decline in the near future. While several countries of the developing world have experienced a substantial decline in fertility in recent years, and a number of others have shown evidence of the beginnings of a decline, high fertility persists in many areas, including those that are most prone to famine. It would be presumptuous to claim an understanding of why fertility has declined where it has and why high fertility has persisted in other areas. These questions are and have been the subject of a great deal of research, and as yet, clear and convincing answers have not been forthcoming. However, recent research suggests that there may be a powerful causal relationship between conditions favorable to the occurrence of famine and the persistence of high fertility.

The scope of the remarks to follow needs to be qualified. They are based on research conducted in Bangladesh and India,[14] and are thus most directly relevant to the situation that pertains in the region of South Asia. It is quite likely that the relationship between threat of famine and fertility holds more generally—in much of Africa, for example—but we can discuss here only the South Asian setting.

The argument, in brief, is that the reproductive behavior of parents is responsive to risk. A high-risk environment is one characterized by a high frequency of events such as natural disasters that threaten normal consumption streams. High-risk environments induce a response of high fertility, or more correctly, create a disincentive to limit natural fertility. The fertility response is not a compensation (or overcompensation) for loss due to infant and child mortality, nor does it reflect irrationality or fatalism on the part of parents. Rather, it reflects the utility of children as a form of insurance against risk. In high-risk environments where alternative forms of insurance are either unavailable or inadequate, the presence of children, particularly mature sons, can be an important determinant of the economic vulnerability of households in times of stress. During crises, mature sons present opportunities for spreading risk and reducing household vulnerability through diversified earnings, temporary migration for work, and as labor reserves in case the principal earner in a household falls ill or dies. In such settings, the role of children in preventing property loss, and perhaps starvation, can create a powerful disincentive to interfere with the natural reproductive process. And in such settings reproduction can be viewed as a kind of self-insurance.

Societies that are currently famine-prone are, by definition, high-risk environments. Famine also signals the absence of adequate risk insurance. Thus, the long-term (or less immediate) demographic response to famine to which we refer is the persistence of high fertility.

Amartya Sen[15] has recently developed a framework for analyzing famines that is useful in considering the risks to which people are exposed in famine-prone areas. Sen focuses on what he calls food entitlements: that is the means by which individuals and families gain access to goods that provide for adequate consumption. He distinguishes between direct entitlement and trade entitlement. Direct entitlement is possessed, for example, by a subsistence cultivator who produces what is necessary for consumption on his own land. Trade entitlement, on the other hand, refers to those who are normally dependent on market purchases or exchange in order to meet consumption needs. Included in this category would be, for example, landless wage laborers, professionals, and salaried persons, and those engaged in craft production or animal husbandry. One can identify another kind of entitlement that fits neatly into neither of these categories but that is important in societies such as Bangladesh, where the economic dependence of women on men is extreme. This might be called "dependent entitlement." Due to a variety of factors, women in rural Bangladesh are denied access to important forms of wage employment and are prohibited from engaging in many activities necessary for agricultural production.[16] The exclusion of women from such activities places them in a position of economic dependence on men. Their food entitlement, therefore, is frequently established through men: husband, father, or son. (Young children in all societies can also be viewed as having this kind of entitlement; women are singled out here because the degree of their dependence on men varies considerably from society to society and it is therefore analytically important, in considering environments of risk, to isolate the special risks that women face as a consequence of their economic dependence.)

Individuals and families are at risk of entitlement failure to different degrees, depending on the basis of their food entitlement and the probability of events or circumstances that threaten particular types of entitlement. For example, weather extremes such as severe flood or drought may cause failure of both direct and trade entitlement. Direct entitlement is threatened by crop failure; while trade entitlement is threatened by depressed labor demand, unemployment, and low wages for the landless. Price inflation unrelated to natural disaster threatens those who rely on trade entitlement, while subsistence framers and others with direct entitlement may remain unaffected. In the case of what was termed dependent entitlement, failure may occur in the event of a husband's death or severe illness, or perhaps divorce.

The 1974 famine in Bangladesh presents an example of failure of all three kinds of entitlement. A severe flood in the summer of 1974 destroyed crops in low-lying areas of the country. Even before the flood, however, Bangladesh was in the grip of hyper-inflation that had seriously eroded the real incomes of the poorer segments of the population. Pockets of famine had been reported in the northwest as early as spring 1974. The flood fueled the inflation of food-grain prices while at the same time causing complete or partial crop failure among cultivators over large areas of the country. The plight of women widowed or abandoned during this period was particularly severe.

Even with this combination of disasters, however, the occurrence of famine was not a necessary consequence. Famine ensued because government and international response was inadequate. The occurrence of modern famine is evidence both of a high-risk environment *and* the absence or failure of risk insurance mechanisms—including public relief.

There are many parts of India that have as harsh a natural environment as rural Bangladesh. One such area is Maharashtra state and the neighboring Telangana region of Andhra Pradesh. To illustrate the potential effectiveness of timely public intervention, we contrast the experience of a village in Bangladesh during the 1974 famine with that of three villages in India that endured the Maharashtra drought of 1970–73 (two of these villages are in Maharashtra and one is in Andhra Pradesh). The severity of these two natural disasters was comparable, and if anything, the Maharashtra drought was the worse of the two. However, governmental response to the disasters differed tremendously, and famine was prevented in the Indian setting. Figure 4 plots the frequency of land sales over time for Char Gopalpur, the Bangladesh village, and the three Indian villages combined. The frequency of distress sale of land is indicative of the response of a community to disaster. The Famine Code of India has long recognized distress sale of land as an early signal of the development of famine conditions. The data in Figure 4 were collected from samples of approximately 120 households in each setting.[17]

Total transactions in a given period of time were standardized by the number of households in existence during the period, that is, by taking as the measure of transaction frequency the number of land sales per eligible household. The figure shows that the frequency of sales in the Bangladesh village has been highly responsive to natural and man-made disasters. The sharp peak during the period 1970–74 reflects a high volume of distress land sales. In contrast to the experience exhibited by the Bangladesh data, the frequency of sale transactions in the combined Indian sample has been low and remarkably constant over time. The absence of distress sales during the Maharashtra drought is striking. In the worst affected of the three villages, 1972–73 brought an almost total cessation of agricultural activity, yet no household in the sample sold land under duress.

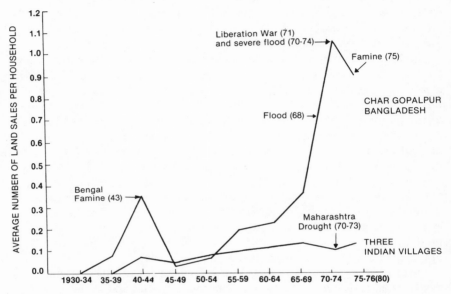

Figure 4. Frequency of land sale transactions in India and Bangladesh

The principal explanation for the contrast in frequency of distress sales evident in Figure 4 is the provision of public relief. Government response to the Maharashtra drought was timely and inspired.[18] The major focus of the relief effort was a massive public-works employment program. A survey of one of the villages during the worst of the drought, 1972–73, indicated that wages from public employment accounted for 46 percent of total income. Since the end of the drought, the Maharashtra State Government has instituted a permanent public employment program (the Maharashtra Employment Guarantee Scheme) that continues to provide a reliable source of employment and wages to all who wish to work. During the flood and famine of 1974–75, no comparable relief effort was undertaken by the government of Bangladesh. Relief was sporadic and confined to the distribution of food and other gratuities.

A closer look at the pattern of land sale and the distribution of famine distress in Char Gopalpur suggests that the resilience of households, the success with which they were able to avoid distress, was closely related to their demographic composition. This was most evident in the case of widows who had no mature sons or other men to depend on during this period. Their fate was uniformly grim. In the Indian villages, on the other hand, widows with no sons, and others who were childless or without mature children, suffered no more than any other segment of the population.

Maharashtra has one of the lowest fertility rates among all states in India, and there is evidence of substantial fertility decline in Maharashtra in recent years. In this setting, it would seem, the diffusion of risk has undermined the economic rationale for high fertility and thus prepared the way toward smaller-sized families. In rural Maharashtra children have become largely redundant as sources of risk insurance. By contrast, Bangladesh has one of the highest and most unyielding fertility rates in all of South Asia. In rural Bangladesh, children retain their importance as sources of security, and parents there have little inducement to limit their fertility.

CONCLUSION

The possibility that famine and rapid population growth perpetuate and feed on one another is, of course, most disturbing. The behavioral response to extreme insecurity—that is, unconstrained reproduction — could have more tragic long-term implications than the more visible and immediate suffering and misery associated with famine mortality. With persistent high fertility and continued rapid population growth, not only is the likelihood of future, perhaps more severe, famines greater than it otherwise would be, but the prospects for true development recede, as government policy is diverted by the effort of feeding a burgeoning population.

Projections, demographic or otherwise, in volatile settings such as Bangladesh, are difficult to make with confidence. It is impossible to imagine that current rates of population growth will persist indefinitely. But it remains uncertain how this growth will be slowed. The recent famine of 1974, despite excess mortality of more than one million, provided no real check to natural increase. With given existing rates of population growth, these deaths were replaced in less than a year. But in the future, it is not inconceivable that famine may provide a more significant "positive check" to natural increase. Rather than achieving rough demographic equilibrium through a decline in fertility as has happened historically in the West, equilibrium could conceivably be achieved through a secular rise in mortality rates, punctuated by the periodic excess mortality of famines.

This bleak scenario is far from inevitable, as can be seen by examining the comparatively favorable experience of Maharashtra State in India. The poverty that one finds there is not dissimilar to what exists in rural Bangladesh. And certainly the environment there is no less harsh with respect to the frequency of natural disasters than that of rural Bangladesh. Yet Maharashtra has been free from famine for the better part of a century and the extraordinarily severe drought of the early 1970s was absorbed with comparatively little distress.

Several important lessons emerge from Maharashtra's experience. First, public response to the drought provides a model of administration and planning for famine relief. An equally important lesson, however, derives from the policy of guaranteed public employment. Through the latter, the government has managed to provide a measure of security in "normal" years, and has shielded individuals from a range of risks whose consequences, while severe, are less dramatic than mass famine. Even in good years there will be a minority of farmers whose crops fail for various reasons, and who may have to resort to the sale of land in order to maintain consumption. There are many other sources of risk with adverse economic consequences, including illness, litigation, theft, and unemployment, that fall far short of the distress caused by famine, which remain a constant threat in rural South Asia.

In settings like Bangladesh, one must add the risks that women face as a consequence of their dependence on men. The behavioral response of fertility to risk is activated not just by the threat of famine, but also by the threat of less dramatic, less widespread kinds of distress that are experienced in ordinary times. Therefore, while the prevention of famine is in itself an important target of policy, it alone is likely to be insufficient to render children redundant as an important source of risk insurance. Children will remain important in this capacity as long as significant risk of loss and insecurity persist in nonfamine years. In order to address the broader policy objective of creating conditions favorable for fertility decline, the goal must be to provide an enduring and institutionalized source of security.

A number of recent famines have occurred in circumstances where aggregate food availability had not declined appreciably from prefamine levels. The Bengal famine of 1943 occurred in such circumstances, as did the Ethiopian famine of 1974.[19] And, indeed, the 1974 famine in Bangladesh cannot be attributed only to decline in food availability. In these cases, the primary cause of famine involved failure of trade entitlement. Famine struck hardest those who are normally dependent on market purchases for food supplies — particularly those whose income depends on wage labor in rural areas. A narrow development strategy of growth in agricultural production, as is currently pursued in Bangladesh, offers precious little security to those whose consumption is based on trade entitlement. Evidence suggests that the proportion of landless and near-landless households is increasing in rural Bangladesh and, thus, the proportion of those whose food entitlement is through trade is also increasing. Moreover, it seems clear that the process of distress sale by which the landless are created is closely related to the environment of risk and the absence of insurance that was described earlier. Against this background, the rationale for adopting a policy goal of broad-based security is clear. It at once addresses the problems of famine, rapid population growth, and economic polarization.

NOTES

1. Mohiuddin Alamgir, *Famine in South Asia* (Cambridge, Mass.: Oelgeschlager, Gunn and Hain, 1980), pp. 85 and 143.

2. Ibid., p. 157.

3. Lincoln Chen and Alauddin Choudhury, "The Dynamics of Contemporary Famine," *Proceedings of the International Population Conference* (Liege, Belgium: International Union for the Scientific Study of Population, 1976), pp. 409–425.

4. Derrick Jeliffe and E. F. Patrice Jeliffe, "The Effects of Starvation on the Function of the Family and of Society," in *Famine: A Symposium Dealing with Nutrition and Relief Operations in Times of Disaster* (Swedish Nutrition Foundation, 1972), pp. 54–63.

5. Z. Stein et al., *Famine and Human Development* (London: Oxford University Press, 1975), p. 92.

6. Chen and Choudhury, "The Dynamics of Contemporary Famine," p. 411.

7. Stein, *Famine and Human Development,* p. 73.

8. A. Antonov, "Children Born during Siege of Leningrad in 1942," *Journal of Pediatrics* 30 (1947): 750–759.

9. John Bongaarts, "Does Malnutrition Affect Fecundity? A Summary of Evidence," *Science* 208 (May 8, 1980): 564–569.

10. Stein, *Famine and Human Development,* p. 83.

11. Ronald Lee, "Short-run Fluctuations in Vital Rates, Prices and Weather," mimeographed, 1979. (Forthcoming as Chapter 9 in E. A. Wrigley and R. Schofield, eds., *The Population History of England 1541–1841*).

12. David Grigg, *Population Growth and Agrarian Change* (Cambridge: Cambridge University Press, 1980), p. 115.

13. Edward J. Clay, "Poverty, Food Insecurity and Public Policy in Bangladesh: Country Case Study for World Development Report IV, 1981" (University of Sussex, Institute of Development Studies, February 1981).

14. Mead Cain, "Risk and Insurance: Perspectives on Fertility and Agrarian Change in India and Bangladesh," *Population and Development Review* 7 (1981): pp. 435–74.

15. Amartya Sen, "Famines," *World Development* 8 (1980): 613–621.

16. Mead Cain, S. R. Khanam, and S. Nahar, "Class, Patriarchy, and Women's Work in Bangladesh," *Population and Development Review* 5 (1979): 405–438.

17. Cain, "Risk and Insurance," pp. 438–39.

18. V. Subramanian, *Parched Earth: The Maharashtra Drought 1970–1973* (Bombay: Orient Longman, 1975).

19. Sen, "Famines" pp. 618–19.

PART III

Ethical Aspects of Famine

There must be a fulcrum on which to balance the reality—past and present—of famine with society's response to such catastrophes. I suggest, in the organization of this book, that the most solid support is an ethical one.

Somehow those with the capacity to share must realize the needs and rights of those with nothing to eat. We must develop a partnership based on principles that transcend national, religious and racial boundaries. To reflect on the why and how and who of this ethical fulcrum I have turned to a distinguished Jesuit scholar and active worker for the world's hungry.

6

WHOSE RIGHT TO FOOD?

William J. Byron, S.J.

Some special challenges are posed by the title of this chapter. What is hoped for here is an ethical reflection on the problem of famine. By famine, I mean epidemic starvation.[1] For a benchmark definition, I refer to geographer William A. Dando, who reviewed famine reports and other writings spanning a period of 6,000 years, and defined famine as "a protracted total shortage of food in a restricted geographical area, causing widespread disease and death from starvation."[2]

What might be suggested by the title of the present essay is the possibility of ethical and unethical famines (ethical, those caused by "acts of God?"; unethical, those caused by acts of war or diplomacy?). It is possible to trace the ethics of the free acts and choices that might be linked along a line of causality leading up to famine. Or, with famine as a given, one might reflect ethically on a human response to a particular famine by those who are not its victims. This latter line of reflection is the one I shall follow. In choosing this route, I acknowledge that I will thus leave unexplored the deepest implication of William Dando's disturbing remark that "natural factors cause crop failures, but humans cause famines." Famines, he flatly asserts, are "man-made."[3]

The notion that famines are man-made is not new. Consider, for instance, the following "famine factors" listed by J. Penkethman in a book published in 1638; it deals with famines in England from that date back to 1066. The work is subtitled *A true relation or Collection of the most remarkable Dearths and Famines which have happened in England since the coming in of William the Conquerer, as also the rising and falling of the price of wheate and other Graine, with the several occasions thereof.* The writer attributes famines in England and Great Britain from 1066 to 1638 to:[4]

1. War, whereby both corn and land were wasted, as also people destroyed.
2. Unseasonable weather, extremes of cold and frost or rain, of winds, thunder, and lightning, tempest, and such like.

William J. Byron, S.J., is president of the University of Scranton and director of Bread for the World.

63

3. The abasing of the coin.
4. Excessive consumption and abuse of wheat and other victuals in voluptuous feasts.
5. The uncharitable greediness or unconscionable hoarding by corn-masters and farmers.
6. The merchants' over-much transporting of grain into foreign parts.

The same writer concludes that the following factors would eliminate famine from the British Isles:

1. Peace, whereby men have liberty to till the ground and reap the fruit thereof.
2. Seasonable and kindly weather.
3. Great store of fine gold and silver.
4. Moderate use of the creature and sparing diet.
5. The corn-masters' and farmers' charitable bounties or conscionable exporting of grain to sale.
6. The importation of grain from foreign parts, through careful control.

Both physical and cultural causes can be found at the roots of famine. The cultural, more influential than the physical throughout the history of famine, present special challenges to ethical reflection. A case-by-case study of famous episodes in the history of famine could build a body of ethical reflection based on sound historical data. The data are available. I think of Cecil Woodham-Smith's *The Great Hunger,* [5] a masterful study of the Irish potato famine of the second half of the decade of the 1840s. In this one volume, the ethician will find abundant data and documentation for reflection on the action or inaction of landlords, British policymakers, and the famished themselves. Trade decisions, dietary habits, ignorance of both agriculture and aquaculture, these and many other cultural factors present themselves for ethical analysis. Similarly, human choices, not natural disaster, were primary causes of the terrible Bengal famine of 1943. The ethical reflection on this great horror in modern Indian history remains to be done.

I intend to approach the ethics of response to famine by two routes: first, by way of the "partnership paradigm" outlined by Francis X. Winters, S.J., and second by way of a "need-care" ethic.

Father Winters, a professor of Christian ethics at Georgetown, is interested in "political morality," which he takes to mean "the effort to universalize (apply to all others) the rights that one demands for oneself." [6] If, for example, the United States claims self-determination as its own right as well as the right of its individual citizens, then the U.S. "is obliged for the sake of consistency to grant this same right of self-determination to all other nations which do not disqualify themselves as partners in the international political system by unjust or expansionist policies." [7] Winters defines partnership as "a relationship of mutual dependence and reciprocal influence." [8] In constructing a "partnership paradigm" as a norm for moral decision making, Winters asserts that "moral wisdom is more liable to be found in one's fellow human beings than in moral principles."[9] Moral principles are, moreover, inadequate without interpretation. Consultation is a prerequisite to decision-making. And consultation should bring the decision-maker into contact with persons rather than with isolated principles.[10]

Those suffering from famine in our world are, indeed, our fellow human beings. Moral wisdom can be drawn from them only if we "consult" them. Our decisions to do or not do something in response to famine depend for their moral quality on our consultation with the famished. Who knows anyone who has "been there" and has not been moved to act?

Representative Benjamin A. Gilman of New York submitted for publication in the *Congressional Record* a report written by a delegation from the Hunger Project after a visit to Somalia, a nation "drowning under a tidal wave of more than a million refugees," as an on-site observer recently described it. One severe but relatively small portion of the problem was the subject of the following section of the report filed by the Hunger Project visitors:[11]

> Once seen it can never be forgotten: more than 76,000 people, 90 percent of them women and children, clustered together on a barren hillside. . . . No one in the camp had received food rations in two days. . . .
>
> The entire water supply for 76,000 people consisted of two shallow, hand-dug wells, each of which had only six inches of murky water remaining. . . .
>
> Thousands of children were infected with measles; thousands more were seriously ill from diseases made worse because of severe malnutrition. Sixty percent of the adults had tuberculosis. There were only two doctors for the entire camp and virtually no medical supplies.
>
> We were witnessing firsthand the worst refugee crisis in the world today: 1.5 million people on the brink of starvation in the East Africa country of Somalia.

The report describes further the famine conditions, caused by years of civil strife and drought, now faced by refugees, ethnic Somalis, who have fled their native lands in the Ogaden region of Ethiopia and have crossed hundreds of miles of desert to Somalia. The problem is devastatingly real to a million and a half of our fellow human beings.

"We returned from East Africa profoundly altered by what we had seen and learned," the Hunger Project delegation reported. They came home with the conviction that the African people "do not seek our charity or pity. Rather they ask for our support and *participation as partners.* "[12]

In what way are we partners with the starving refugees in Somalia? This may be a contemporary way of asking, "And who is my neighbor?" (Luke 10:29).

Recall that partnership is a relationship of "mutual dependence and reciprocal influence." Our tendency is to read the relationship one way. They depend on us. How can we be said to be dependent on them? Similarly, we presume that we can, perhaps should, have influence there. But how can they have influence here? *Mutual* dependence and *reciprocal* influence presuppose a two-way street. What are the starving Africans asking when they ask for our "participation as partners," in the words of the Hunger Project report? Are the starving Africans opening up for us today a source of moral wisdom which we, by failing to consult, may easily ignore?

Arthur Jones, former editor and now diplomatic correspondent for the *National Catholic Reporter*, has written a series of articles on the famine in Somalia for that newspaper.[13] In his fifth dispatch, Jones quotes the views of an unidentified "European with more than forty years' administrative and medical experience in Africa: Sudan, Ethiopia, Nigeria, Libya, Somalia, and Kenya." Jones adds that others he has met with who had extensive relief and development experience in the Third World share the following views:[14]

> I believe it is morally wrong for us to treat Third World nations this way. We should treat them like adults, or at least like late adolescents and allow them — not us — to make the mistakes in their country and to suffer the consequences of their own mistakes.

It is assumed that we should indeed respond to famine conditions with direct relief and assistance. The quality, the moral quality, of our response is the issue here. There is an accompanying assumption that the appropriate moral response will also provide a more workable relief effort than the well-intentioned but unsuccessful efforts attempted thus far. I endorse none of the judgments Arthur Jones makes elsewhere in his dispatches about the effectiveness of service provided by the United Nations and the "Volags," the many voluntary agencies at work in Somalia. I do, however, find in his journalistic critique and in the scholarly analyses of others who have written on famine[15] a basis for arguing that a poorly organized relief response to famine is, in fact, an unethical response. There is a seductive charm in the dictum that anything worth doing is worth doing poorly. Radical analysis of the problem of world poverty in terms of ideologically grounded patterns of domination and dependency suggests, however, that inept relief efforts not only fail the famished but deprive the disadvantaged, dependent nation of the exercise of power which would, in turn, develop the competence and confidence needed to move the nation toward more self-reliant development.

If we are, in fact, partners with the famished, in a relationship of "mutual dependence and reciprocal influence" with them, we must, first of all, trust them. We must next listen to them and be prepared to free them to use resources we provide in ways they judge best suited to their needs, their environment, and their culture. If we listen to them, we permit them to influence us. If we turn over to them resources to be used by them for their relief, we become dependent on them for the success of our response! We thus admit them to full partnership. We establish an ethical relationship.

At the beginning of this essay, I borrowed Francis A. Winters' idea of political morality, namely, the political readiness to apply to all others the rights that one demands for oneself. In 1976, the U.S. Congress adopted a "Right-to-Food" resolution declaring the right of every human being to a "nutritionally adequate diet," and that this right is "henceforth to be recognized as a cornerstone of United States policy." This is a human right, not a right conditioned by citizenship. If we believe in, and assert for ourselves, a right to food, then we should acknowledge that all others have this right. We should also work to assist others, particularly the famished, in realizing this right where those famished others do not remove themselves from partnership with us in the international political system. And even in those special cases, we should readily distinguish between suffering people and regimes which rule them while refusing partnership with us. To the extent we can, we ought to help.

Why should we help? Because the famished have a clear need and we have a capacity to meet that need. It is an instance, in the international community, of a need-care ethic which is commonplace in interpersonal relationships. If the needy person is within my sight and reach, and if my capacity to care corresponds at all with that person's need, then a need-care ethic binds the two of us in a relationship of mutual dependence and reciprocal influence. By refusing to care, I diminish my humanity. By responding to need, I become more fully human. The need-care ethic fits well within the partnership paradigm. Each of these ethical constructs is useful now in the face of famine. But those of us with the capacity to care, the affluent, can choose to go the route of privatization. We can withdraw.

In *The Private Future*, Martin Pawley writes:

> Western society is on the brink of collapse — not into crime, violence, or madness or redeeming revolution, as many would believe — but into withdrawal. Withdrawal from the whole system of values and obligations that has historically been the basis of public, community and family life. Western societies are collapsing not from an assault on their most cherished values, but from a voluntary, almost enthusiastic abandonment of them by people who are learning to live private lives of an unprecedented completeness with the aid of the momentum of a technology which is evolving more and more into a pattern of socially atomizing appliances.[16]

Language like that is helpful in reminding us that we have problems too. The famished can help us if only we bring ourselves to help them.

In my view, a genuine human need constitutes a genuine human right. The human right derives from the human need. I also think the capacity to care for a genuine human need in another constitutes, in the person with potential to care, a genuine human obligation. The seriousness of the moral obligation depends on the seriousness of the need and on the proximity and capability of the person (or the person together with the others with whom he or she associates in community, including the national community) to meet the need. The relevance of these considerations to the problem of famine in our world will not be noted until the problem of famine is itself seen by those not directly touched by it.

Joined with care in a need-care ethic must be the notion of competence. It must not be simply implied but made quite explicit that the capacity to care refers to competent care. A poorly organized famine-relief program is an unethical response. Failure of one competent relief agency to coordinate with another competent relief agency addressing the same famine situation is, in fact, an ethical failure for both agencies. To care, add competence; and to both of them, add coordination. Each is an ethical issue.

Another issue, worthy of ethical reflection, is the complicated relationship of food deficits resulting from ecological damage produced by an exploitative system of ownership and use of resources, particularly land. In this one issue, ethical analysis can examine both the "tragedy of the commons" and the excesses of private ownership. Such reflection, unsupported by data and unaided by historical, cultural, and scientific analysis, will be of little value. Such reflection will, moreover, raise serious ethical questions about comparative economic systems.

I have tried up to this point to stay within the range of reflection specified at the outset, namely, the ethics of a response to famine. I want now to say more about famine types and places of famine potential, and do this with attention to both physical and cultural causes as evidenced in the course of history. This will be schematic and brief. It will be totally dependent on the work of William Dando.

Dando identifies five basic famine types: (1) physical, (2) transportation, (3) cultural, (4) political, and (5) overpopulation.[17] The last has an economic dimension which surely requires attention. That dimension raises the question of the distribution, as opposed to the production, of food and wealth.

Adding spatial considerations to his five types, and running them through a long span of history, Dando lists:[18]

1. Physical (or Egyptian) famines in regions where the physical environment was naturally hostile to intensive forms of sedentary agriculture but man developed techniques which enabled him to temper natural hazards in all but their extreme form.
2. Transportation (or Roman) famines in highly urbanized, commercial, or industrial food-deficit regions dependent upon distant food sources and supplied normally by a well-developed transportation system.
3. Cultural (or West European) famines in food-surplus regions induced by archaic social systems, cultural practices, and overpopulation.
4. Political (or Eastern European) famines in regions that are nominally self-sufficient in basic foodstuffs but where regional politics or regional politi-

cal systems determine food production, food distribution, and food availability.

5. Overpopulation (or Asian) famines in drought-prone or flood-prone, overpopulated, marginal agricultural regions with primitive agricultural systems, whose inhabitants' perennial food intake was only slightly above starvation levels.

Turning then to the potential for famine in our time, and employing his "types" referenced to geographic areas, Dando suggests[19] that Type 1, the physical, is no longer a serious causal contender. Recall that droughts are natural, but famines are man-made. Type 2, transportation and communication factors, could create real problems in drought-prone regions like the Sahel, and also, as we are witnessing today, in Ethiopia-Somalia-Yemen. Cultural, or Type 3 factors, which inhibit agricultural productivity, are likely to combine with population pressures to produce serious food problems in the Caribbean area. Political activities (Type 4) have famine-producing potential in Transjordan-Syria as well as in the Ethiopia-Somalia-Yemen areas. And over-population (Type 5) in areas of marginal agriculture and severe natural hazards in Pakistan, India, Bangladesh, Burma, and Laos raises the specter of famine while calling for decisions on resettlement, birth control, and comprehensive economic development. Our lopsided world is already in a race with famine.

It is certain that famine, which means epidemic starvation, is the inevitable future for millions of our fellow human beings on our planet in our time. This places upon each of us an immediate ethical challenge. The immediacy of our response, a relief response characterized by care, competence, coordination, and communication, must not be permitted to absolve or distract us from the deeper and more difficult ethical challenge. I refer to the need to increase food production in the food-deficit nations. This is the single most important issue of our time; its only real rival for top rank on any apocalyptic list of world problems is the threat of a nuclear holocaust.

What can we do? What must we do? Widespread (worldwide) attitudinal change is an indispensable first step. Individuals (you and I) are responsible for our own attitudes. Individuals (you and I) can assist and encourage attitudinal change in others. This I take to be the task of education, opinion formation, and communication, hence of scholars, schools, journalists, and communicators.

An aware and attitudinally receptive world community might then be encouraged to follow the critical path of factors identified by J. Penkethman as necessary to eliminate famine from the British Isles in 1638.[20] With appropriate updating to our circumstances, the list, which I quoted at the beginning of the essay, can set an agenda for our day.

First, "peace, whereby men have liberty to till the ground and reap the fruit thereof" puts both land reform and the arms race on our famine agenda, not to mention diplomatic peace-keeping pursuits.

Second, "seasonable and kindly weather" invites the application of science and technology to our problem. Perhaps the weather will always elude our control, but it need not elude our understanding or our capacity to adjust and adapt.

Third, "great store of fine gold and silver" suggests the need for a sound and fair international monetary system where rich and poor nations alike participate fully and by the same rules.

Fourth, "moderate use of the creature and sparing diet" reminds the affluent inhabitants of our global village that they have to settle for less in order that their disadvantaged fellow human beings might have more, or, at the very least, not face famine while others enjoy abundance.

Fifth, "the corn-masters' and farmers' charitable bounties or conscionable exporting of grain to sale" tells us that export cropping must be managed wisely, agricultural labor must receive a fair return, and agricultural planning is important to a sound economy. For such planning to be effective it must be accompanied by the establishment of an international system of grain reserves.

Sixth, "the importation of grain from foreign parts, through careful control" puts trade on the famine agenda.

This agenda outline admits of much more detail. Specialists in political, economic, historical, biological, cultural, and specifically agricultural considerations might easily add useful agenda for both prevention and relief of famine. It is the ethicists' task to keep these considerations on the agenda of individuals and nations in the world community. Nothing is more important for our time.

NOTES

1. Josue de Castro, *The Geography of Hunger* (Boston: Little, Brown, 1952), pp. 5, 23; cited by William A. Dando, *The Geography of Famine* (New York: Halstead Press, Wiley, 1980), p. 60.

2. William A. Dando, "Six Millennia of Famine: Map and Model," *Proceedings of the Association of American Geographers,* vol. 8 (1976), p. 20.

3. Dando, *The Geography of Famine*, p. viii.

4. See J. Penkethman, *Artachthos or a New Book Declaring the Assise of Bread* (London: R. Bishop & Edward Griffine, 1638), p. 13; quoted by William A. Dando, The Geography of Famine, p. 122.

5. Cecil B. Woodham-Smith, *The Great Hunger: Ireland 1845-1849* (London: Hamish Hamilton, and New York: Harper and Row, 1963; London: New English Library, and New York: Signet, 1974).

6. Francis X. Winters, *Politics and Ethics* (New York: Paulist Press, 1975), p. 95.

7. Ibid.

8. Ibid., p. 12.

9. Ibid., p. 3.

10. Traditional Roman Catholic morality would have the decision-maker consult authority. Traditional Protestant morality would direct the consultation in a horizontal fashion to the reciprocal influence of church members (or members of the larger civil society) on one another. The point to be noted is that both traditions include consultation. (See Winters, *Politics and Ethics,* pp. 4-5.)

11. "The Urgent Need for Humanitarian Assistance to Somalia," *Congressional Record* (March 3, 1981), p. E788.

12. Ibid., p. E789. (Emphasis added.)

13. *National Catholic Reporter:* " 'Drought, Refugees, War, UN Bungling Devastate Famine-Wracked Somalia' " (March 20, 1981);"Somalia Relief Reveals 'UN Response Confused' " (March 27, 1981); " 'Third World Poverty Made Easy: Beggars and Bums' " (April 3, 1981); "Exploring 'Several Faces' of Somalia's Christianity" (April 10, 1981); "Aid Makes Third World 'a Greedy, Spoiled Child' " (April 17, 1981); " 'Most of All, Refugees Suffer' from UN 'Bungling, Waste' " (April 24, 1981).

14. *National Catholic Reporter,* April 17, 1981, p. 3.

15. See the bibliographic references in Richard W. Franke and Barbara H. Chasin, *Seeds of Famine* (Montclair, N.J.: Allanheld, Osmun 1980), pp. 240–256; see also footnote references in Dando, *Geography of Famine.*

16. Martin Pawley, *The Private Future,* (New York: Random House, 1974), p. 8.

17. Dando, *The Geography of Famine,* p. 87.

18. Ibid.

19. Ibid., p. 90.

20. See above Note 4.

PART IV

The Economics of Famine

Supply and demand, productivity and distribution, yields and per capita measurements are the phrases economists use to analyze and interpret—and occasionally predict—the patterns of a society. In this section four internationally known economists express a cautious optimism for the future feeding of the human race.

They build their vision on a review of the history of famine, as well as on recent trends in the Third World. A common theme in each chapter is the belief that any change in the nutritional status of poor people will depend more on man's actions—or inactions—than on the vagaries of nature.

Our four economists were not selected merely as masters of theoretical monetary policy, but because each has worked extensively in the Third World and has contributed to our understanding of the unique fiscal problems that plague emerging nations.

7

OPPORTUNITY IN THE FACE OF DISASTER— REVIEW OF THE ECONOMIC LITERATURE ON FAMINE

Mark Perlman

There are usually two sides to any contribution toward the understanding of events. One is theoretical; the other is factual. The theoretical approach can provide powerful tools; the ultimate test, however, is not simply the quality of the tools, but the ways these powerful tools are employed in concrete or specific situations. Thus, the economic contribution includes abstraction (necessary for the development of the analytical tools) and historical generalization.

What is famine? Simply put, famine is so severe a shortage of food that persons' lives are significantly shortened or stunted. A brief review of history suggests that famine occurs in many ways. Two of these ways claim our immediate attention. One is unanticipated disaster such as acute food shortages following an earthquake, military disaster, widespread destructive flooding, or the consequence of parasitical infestation of crops or human beings. Another kind of famine involves an endemic shortage of food, where the land is unable to provide sufficient sustenance for all the land's population or for some segments of it. One difference separating these two kinds of famine is tied to society's capacity to plan avoidance of a famine.

Whatever knowledge there is about both catastrophe-famine and chronic endemic famine, that knowledge must be understood in terms of actual experiences. To be forewarned, as was the case in Joseph's Egypt, is often enough. Seven years of warning permitted the construction and maintenance of a granary system sufficient not only to tide over the domestic and some temporary populations in Egypt, but also permitted Joseph's master, the Pharaoh, to capture much of the power and most of the wealth in Egypt. In catastrophe-famine, the great problem is not only misery and death, it is also the redistribution of wealth and power.

Mark Perlman is professor of economics, University of Pittsburgh and managing editor, *Journal of Economic Literature*.

In recent decades the usual examples of catastrophe-famine are the destruction wrought by World War II, the Vietnam War and its Cambodian consequences, certain local earthquake situations, and the like.

In the case of Joseph, the creation of granary reserves was sufficient. And it is not unusual for societies to accumulate stores of food sufficient to cover the disaster period. While many examples of this planning are available, certainly medieval Byzantium, with its vast storehouses of grain and great cisterns, stands out as exemplar.

Presumably, the catastrophic form of famine occurs "out of the blue." Some catastrophes are regular, and steps like flood control or irrigation mitigate them. For that reason, individuals and nations often create plans or reserves. Reserves of food and reserves of drinking water are clearly the answer that the economist suggests.

But these reserves may not always prove sufficient because the catastrophe is of greater scope than anticipated; the rains seem "never" to come as in the case of the current sub-Sahara drought, the temperature "never" seems to warm up as in the case of the series of green winters of 1812–1819,[1] or the Irish potato blight that spread and persisted beyond anyone's wildest expectations.[2]

What these events have in common is not the unexpected onset of a disaster, but a combination of its awfulness and its duration. My point is that *some* catastrophe-famines are anticipated, and to be forewarned is to be forearmed. But such is not always the case.

There is in current economic theory much concern with *uncertainty*, that is, with coping with the unknown. One school of thought, led by the Nobel laureate Herbert Simon, believes that with enough experience one ought to be able to create reserves for most things—the only drawbacks being that one cannot always insure for certain kinds of disasters because the costs of information and/or of the creation of reserves are just too great.[3] Another school of thought, that often associated with G. L. S. Shackle, believes that one can never plan with adequate effectiveness because the future is "kaleidoscopic." There will be a sufficient number of unique events dwarfing anyone's recollection of past experiences and change is itself relentless. The reserves brought up to do battle in one hour will be in the wrong place and of the wrong type to do battle in the next. In Shackle's view, reason (based on experience and logical rules of thinking) and time are polar extremes. Reason may serve as a basis, a system of reserves, but time has a way of rendering human anticipations irrelevant.[4]

In practice, however, most individuals compete and when catastrophe-famines occur, generally they have been and can be handled by part, if not all, of the population. It is the speed with which individuals react and react again which is the saving factor for "the most adaptable."[5]

However, it is not with catastrophe-famines, but with chronic endemic famines, that economists come up with their best set of insights. Chronic or endemic famines are situations occurring where year after year, decade after decade, hunger stalks the land. The insufficiency of food in this instance is not to be seen simply as the result of a one-time disaster, but as a result of policy choices. This kind of continuing chronic or endemic famine has been one of the principal interests in the development of the economics discipline. This kind of situation has existed until now in many less developed countries. This kind of situation has become institutionalized in contemporary Cambodia. This kind of situation also threatens the economies of industrialized nations such as Poland. To understand the economists' approach, it is probably wise to go back a couple of centuries before the period of the European industrialization when chronic or endemic famine was also there the rule.

The history of modern industrialization starts with two "revolutions," which occurred prior to the Industrial Revolution itself. These two were revolutions in agricultural production and transportation. Both were prerequisites to the great growth of population in Great Britain during the eighteenth century, which in turn was the critical change.

Interestingly enough, a theoretical explanation of the situation in sixteenth-century Europe was supplied by a contemporary Italian writer, Giovanni Botero, in his book *Della grandezza della città* (1588).[6] Botero's book explained how the relative shortage of food (as expressed in rising food prices) kept cities from expanding indefinitely. What Botero had to say was somewhat inverted because he clearly suggested that by coming to grips with the uses of technology (particularly with regard to transportation) food shortages could be minimized. Botero did not use the term infrastructure, but that is today's term. What were and are these infrastructure additions?

Within a century and a half of Botero's time what has been termed the great agricultural revolution was underway. Jethro Tull and Robert Bakewell introduced the basis of modern agronomy and modern animal husbandry. The two great breakthroughs involved the use of turnips and maize (corn) fodder and the selective breeding of cattle.[7]

Most economists and economic historians believe that this agricultural revolution occurred about the same time that there was a transportation revolution. The latter involved the construction of a vast network of canals as well as improved roads. The names of the great canal builders are little known; however, Thomas Telford and Robert McAdam were the great innovators in road building. Later, of course, Stephenson's invention of the locomotive engine introduced the railroad age.[8]

These agricultural and transportation revolutions were dramatic changes in infrastructure. The Industrial Revolution occurred afterwards and seems to have become possible mainly because of the two prior occurrences.

When Arnold Toynbee (the elder) gave his five *Lectures on the Industrial Revolution*,[9] his major point was that sustaining the eighteenth-century growth in population required capital substitution for expanding production. But more happened; not only did populations survive but real living standards rose. Food and other consumables became more plentiful.

If one is comfortable dating the Industrial Revolution with the invention of the steam engine (1776), then that is also the date of the development of modern economics, with the publication of Adam Smith's *Wealth of Nations*. It was not Smith, however, who introduced modern economic analysis. T. R. Malthus and particularly David Ricardo are generally credited with this change. Classical economics started with Malthus' worries about endemic famine facing the burgeoning population; Ricardo's policy solutions involved international specialization (which for England meant the production of manufactured goods and the importation of food). Ricardo's law of comparative advantage (efficiency-consciousness in this regard) was probably correct. Malthus had doubts about relying on foreign sources for food, but Ricardo's group won. Not only were the Corn Laws ultimately repealed (thus ending protection for the British farmer), but, more importantly, the import of food introduced an era of food plenty in Britain.

Like so many of today's development economists, the classical economists, particularly as their views were summarized by Nassau Senior, believed that population would burgeon, that real wage rates would advance reasonably little, if at all, that there were decreasing returns to agriculture, and that there were increasing returns to manufacturing.

Were the classical economists wrong? In reality, they were. Population did not grow at anywhere near the rate they anticipated. Much to their surprise, real wage rates grew at generally ever-increasing velocities, and, most of all, their pessimistic view about agriculture operating in an area of decreasing returns was shown to be not only an error in direction but also devoid of any perception of what could and would happen. They were right about the rate of increase of manufacturing output; had they applied the same reasoning to agriculture, their contribution would have been fully useful.

It is precisely because so many contemporary development economists have embraced the classical economists' error regarding the capacity to increase agricultural output that the advice given by most development economists since World War II has generally been counterproductive. This advice was quickly grasped by those less developed countries which dreamed of steel mills, auto factories, and nuclear technology.

The great example of agriculture operating in areas of increasing returns is the American experience since 1935. In the mid-1930s there was not only a tremendous agricultural surplus in the United States, but the unit price of farm goods was falling drastically. When Franklin Roosevelt first became president of the United States (1933), he sought and got legislation which restricted agricultural output. That legislation was declared unconstitutional. Thereafter, he sought and received legislation which directed that the amount of land used for agricultural output was to be curtailed. In order to protect farmers' incomes his legislation provided a system of price supports. Farmers facing the market were thus enjoined from using all of their land for production, but they were permitted to increase inputs on the fields which they tilled. These inputs involved better fertilizers, better seeds, better plowing, and irrigation. Because farmers were guaranteed reasonably high unit prices for the goods they produced, they had no incentive to restrict production. On the contrary, the more they produced, the more they earned.

The result was, of course, a vast surplus in the latter years of the 1930s. But this disappeared during World War II. After World War II, the surplus recurred and the American federal government undertook to distribute the bounty to needy nations, first among the destroyed industrialized nations in Europe and Asia and later among the impecunious less developed countries.

So much has been written about the unanticipated effects of price supports on the growth of American agricultural output that other historical American policies have been neglected. Originally, American railroads, trying to sell the land which had been given to them in return for their laying of tracks, offered expert guidance to immigrant farmers in order to make the transition from Europe to the American Midwest easy and rapid. By the turn of the century the various states, particularly those with established agricultural schools, had taken over these local programs and were instructing the young farmers themselves, and were coordinating their efforts with the field agents in every county. After World War I, the federal government took over the county agent program. Thus, the incentive system offered by the New Deal Agricultural Adjustment Act supplemented the already present educational and research infrastructure. In other words the wealth of the American example is the existence of a set of infrastructures, an understanding of the importance of increasing productivity in food production and a perception of the efficacy of incentive systems.

Such has not been the experience of the less developed countries, particularly in those with endemic famine. Many of these, in trying to industrialize, rapidly offered incentives to urban manufacturing through food-price ceilings; in reality, they were presenting the peasantry with disincentives. Agricultural development in these countries was generally discouraged. That industrialized nations like the United States or Denmark or Holland were agricultural exporters was quickly forgotten; instead, these less developed countries wanted simply to be exporters of manufactured goods. The fetish for manufacturing goods combined with a reluctance to use any kind of profit maximizing incentive, upon which the Roosevelt Administration stumbled, led to the great endemic famine problem in some of these countries. Their reluctance to allow the price of food to rise sufficiently has resulted in the relocation of resources to urban and manufacturing development from rural areas and food production.

From an analytical standpoint, therefore, the kind of argument provided by Professor D. Gale Johnson in his paper in this symposium has more than a political or a curiosity role. Stressed in the great writings in agricultural economics is the importance of adequate prices, however paid, going to the agricultural sector. The present emphasis on importance of "cheap" prices for food for the urban sector, whatever else one wants to believe, is not as important in the long haul as pursuing policies yielding adequate prices in the agricultural sector. If the latter policy is adopted, the ultimate result may be cheap food in the urban communities. If, on the contrary, one starts with cheap food in the urban communities (by virtue of price controls or price subsidies), one rarely ends up with sufficient food to prevent endemic starvation.

The theory of how to deal with chronic endemic shortages involves several parts:

1. The development of a concept of regional specialization for economic activity so that areas best fitted for food production concentrate on that activity.
2. The realization that incentive systems used to encourage efficiency in specialization in the manufacturing sector can also be used to do the same things in the agricultural sector.
3. A systematic willingness to increase efficiency in production and distribution of food.

The title of this chapter suggests that famine presents opportunities. Why? Because famine is the kind of disaster which encourages people to reconsider in the most basic sense what their priorities are, what is hampering their achievements, and the importance of learning from other people's experiences.

At the outset I suggested that wisdom consists of knowing something about facts and history as well as the capacity to develop analyses or systematic insights. The literature on famine, as I noted initially, can be divided in several ways. I find the distinction between catastrophe-famine and chronic or endemic famine useful. While I am not sure that all catastrophe-famines can be averted, the record shows that wise policies can mitigate their effects. As for chronic or endemic famine, the important analytical insights are (1) the necessity of revolutions in such infrastructures as agricultural production, transportation, research, and education; (2) the recognition that the future of many societies does not rest on the mistaken notion of manufacturing as being economically wiser than agriculture; (3) that incentive systems have been used successfully in the agricultural sector, particularly the American case, and (4) that appropriate pricing and individual rewards in the agricultural sector could serve to cure most of the chronic or endemic famine currently existing.

NOTES

1. John D. Post, *The Last Great Subsistence Crisis in the Western World* (Baltimore and London: Johns Hopkins University Press, 1977).
2. Cecil Woodham-Smith, *The Great Hunger: Ireland 1845–1849* (London: Hamish Hamilton, and New York: Harper & Row, 1963; London: New English Library, New York: Signet, 1974).
3. Herbert A. Simon, *Administrative Behavior: A Study of Decision-Making Processes in Administrative Organization* (1947), 3rd ed. expanded (New York: Macmillan and Free Press;

London: Collier Macmillan, 1976); "Rationality as Process and as Product of Thought," *American Economic Review* 68 (1978): 1–16.

4. George L. Shackle, *Epistemics and Economics: A Critique of Economic Doctrine* (New York and London: Cambridge University Press, 1973); *Keynesian Kaleidics: The Evolution of a General Political Economy* (Edinburgh: Edinburgh University Press, 1974); *Imagination and the Nature of Choice* (Edinburgh: Edinburgh University Press, 1979).

5. Cf. Theodore W. Schultz, "The Value of the Ability to Deal with Disequilibria," *Journal of Economic Literature* 13 (1975): 827–46.

6. Giovanni Botero, *La grandezza della città* (1588), trans. as *The Greatness of Cities* by R. Peterson (London, 1606).

7. J. L. and Barbara Hammond, *The Rise of Modern Industry* (1925), (Evanston: Harper Torch Books, 1969), pp. 66–80.

8. Ibid., pp. 81–96.

9. Arnold Toynbee, *Lectures on the Industrial Revolution* (London, 1884).

8

SPREADING THE GREEN REVOLUTION

Sudhir Sen

I find myself in a rather privileged position in this distinguished gathering. With one possible exception I am the only "waschechter" or washproof Third-Worlder among the speakers. With your indulgence I shall therefore be reasonably blunt in my presentation. The phenomenon of famine, or the threat of it, does not permit too many euphemisms.

In January, 1981 the much-esteemed *Bulletin of the Atomic Scientists* moved the hands of its "doomsday clock" from seven to four minutes before the midnight of extinction. The step was prompted by a new arms race recently unleashed with improved missile accuracy and mobility, signalling the acceptance of counterforce first-strike by both sides. It was a grim reminder of the fateful times we live in.

Another clock with awesome implications has been ticking for quite some time—that of global famine. No trained hands have fashioned it to match the *Bulletin's* handiwork and to adjust its movements. However, fourteen years ago the Paddock brothers did make an attempt, albeit a clumsy one, in their hair-raising *Famine 1975!*[1] And around the same time we saw the emergence of a group of scientists preaching the gospel of triage. They used their considerable talents not to find out how hungry nations could be saved from the jaws of famine, but to determine the precise order in which they should be sacrificed. They advocated surrender to the enemy without firing a single shot.

But the Green Revolution had just burst on the horizon. It mocked the cynicism of the doomsayers. And most of us felt confident that with this rapidly unfolding revolution we would be able to beat back the looming famine.

Those hopes have remained largely unfulfilled. All we have done so far is to buy some extra time—a decade or two. The specter of famine has been far from ostracized. In fact, famine is now raging in all its fury in Northeast Africa, where tribal warfare and superpower rivalry superimposed on a

Sudhir Sen is the former director at the U.N.D.P.

drought-stricken primitive agriculture have created a ghastly tragedy. For the first time we have seen the ugly face of triage in the Horn of Africa, where too many people are too close to death and there is not enough food to go round.

Nor should we forget the 800 million people, or one-fifth of humanity, whom Robert McNamara calls the "absolute poor." Their absolute number is still rising as population leaps ahead. They live in famine and near-famine conditions, spread over the Third World, especially in Central Africa and South Asia. The reality of famine is already there, even though we fight shy of the word as a matter of semantics or as a sop to our conscience.

After surveying the precarious world food situation, Food and Agriculture Organization (FAO) Director-General Edouard Saouma recently sounded the alarm. "We are really in a state of general alert," he declared. Here are some of the facts he cited. The rate of agricultural production has not kept pace with population growth in very many countries of the Third World. In fifteen countries, production in 1979 was even lower than in 1970; twenty-nine developing countries are now suffering from acute food shortage; the situation is particularly serious in Africa, where people have 10 percent less food than they had ten years ago and where starvation is imminent.

World grain production, according to FAO's estimate for 1980–1981, would drop by six million tons. The results are clear: declining stocks, rising prices, greater dependence of the food-deficit countries on external sources. The import requirements of developing countries in 1981, according to Dr. Saouma, might reach 94 million tons of grain. Where would they get this huge tonnage from? And how would they pay for it? Prices were already exorbitant, and are still trending upwards. Wheat prices, for example, had gone up 30 percent by early 1981. And developing nations were already staggering under an external debt burden of more than $360 billion.

For the third year in succession world grain stocks were expected to decline—by the end of the 1980–1981 season they would probably total just 14 percent of world consumption, which is well below the minimum deemed necessary for world food security. This means we continue to be vulnerable to the vagaries of climate. And unless the 1981 harvests are good, the world may experience another crisis similar to that of 1973, or worse.

Such, then, are the dismal prospects that face us today. And so the question arises: What happened to the Green Revolution on which we had built our hopes not so very long ago? Has its promise faded—for good? And will the apocalyptic vision of the Paddock brothers and the triagists, after all, come true with a slight delay—this year, or in the Orwellian year of 1984, or a bit later?

For answers to these questions it is essential to look back and set the perspective right, also to grasp the real meaning of the Green Revolution and assess the prospects it holds for the future.

For a correct diagnosis of today's problems we have to ask ourselves a straight question: how did we manage to arrive at today's dreadful mess, with population constantly threatening to outrun food production and setting the stage for hunger and starvation on a mindboggling scale? What, in short, has actually gone wrong? Economists, sociologists, scientists, politicians, and others are of course ready with their own answers; and quite a few would still hark back to the past and flog a dead horse called colonialism. Almost all of them are quite off the mark. The world food crisis is essentially a postcolonial and post-World War II phenomenon. It stems not from coldblooded exploitation of people, but from a lopsided application of science; not from the folly of individual nations, but from the collective folly of human-kind.

Here is a revealing episode that occurred in New York just over forty years ago, in February 1941, although it is buried deep in the archives beyond the reach even of the most penetrating minds. The Rockefeller Foundation was about to develop a program of assistance for Mexico. And so Raymond B. Fosdick, the then president of the Foundation, approached Henry A. Wallace for his advice. By then Mr. Wallace was well on his way to realizing one of his favorite dreams, namely, to put a chicken in every household pot. The advice he gave was both forthright and apropos. It would be "a fine thing" if they went to Mexico, he told Mr. Fosdick, but warned that "they should not do much in the way of health work" because he thought *"it would be a crime to make another Puerto Rico out of Mexico with population crowding on the means of subsistence."*

He also told Mr. Fosdick: *"The all-important thing was to expand the means of subsistence.* The corn of Mexico was yielding only 10 bushels to the acre. The principal source of food among the Mexican masses was corn. Above everything there, a job should be done on increasing the yield of corn. I know positively that a very great improvement could be made."[2]

Soon afterward the Foundation sent three leading American scientists to Mexico to carry out a quick reconnaissance and feasibility study. And this led, a few months later, to the establishment of a grain genetics program under Dr. J. George Harrar, later president of the Foundation. So began a program that, by the 1960s, culminated in the Green Revolution, though for some fortuitous reasons, the pride of place went to wheat rather than corn.

The point at issue is this: Since World War II the developing countries have received, in one form or another, a great deal of assistance in health and tropical medicine, while tropical agriculture has suffered from chronic and cruel neglect. The World Health Organization (WHO) has set a spectacular record of achievements, virtually stamping out malaria (even though it threatens to reemerge in some pockets) and other arch-killers; it has far out-shone FAO in performance. Bilateral programs, too, have made large contri-butions to that end. And the transnational corporations have spread the biomedical revolution far and wide with a dazzling array of wonder drugs and medical technologies. The result has been a rapid extension of life expec-tancies, leading to an explosive growth of population in the developing world at a time when its food production remained stagnant or lagged way behind.

Thus, we have done precisely what Henry Wallace had warned the aid-givers not to do. As a result, population has relentlessly crowded on the means of subsistence, threatening to deliver two billion people or more to perpetual hunger and starvation. In a figurative sense, we have made of the Third World a vast "Puerto Rico" of the kind Henry Wallace, in his prescient wisdom, was most anxious to avoid.

The world food crisis, at bottom, is a man-made phenomenon. It is the direct outcome of topsy-turvy priorities, of the health-before-food, or health-without-food approach, of boosting longevity without paying heed to the adequacy of life-sustaining nutrition, of saving the masses of people from mass killers only to deliver them to mass starvation. No wonder that "development has not developed"; in fact, it was derailed right at the start. Having mindlessly unleashed the demographic genie we are now frantically looking for some magic means to bring it under control. Some, in cold desperation, have gone the length of advocating triage, man's ultimate inhumanity to man!

When the food problem began to attract more attention in the early fifties, we immediately ran into formidable snags. First, there was a widespread misperception even among experts. They believed that a very rapid improvement in food production could be brought about in the poor nations, and that all they needed to do so were men, money, and machinery. They were the so-called "know-how show-how enthusiasts" who believed hybrid corn could be transplanted overnight, say, from Kansas State to the Ganges Valley, just as a steel mill or a textile plant could be hauled across the oceans and established in a developing country. What they overlooked was a simple fact, namely: that agriculture deals with plants and animals, which are living things and therefore not easily transferable across climatic barriers; that they call for specific research in a given environment for their improvement, propagation, and protection. The experts needed some rude shocks before they realized this simple truth. By contrast, medical experts have all along regarded it as an axiom that an effective system of tropical medicine for controlling tropical diseases can be developed only on the basis of intensive research and investigations on the spot.

Today we know better. Improved varieties of crops and breeds of animals constitute the heart of agricultural development. Hence the emphasis now being laid on crop and animal research in the tropics to fill a critical void inherited from the past.

The other snag was the huge food surplus in the United States. What could be more reasonable for Americans, as they looked at their mounting stockpile of food at home and pervasive hunger abroad, than to urge a marriage of the two? It looked like an ideal solution, good for the pocket and good for the soul. So began a phase of humanitarian dumping of highly subsidized food in the developing countries. The first voice of reason to challenge this policy came from Theodore Schultz, who was awarded the Nobel prize three years ago. The U. S. policy, he argued, was unsound for its own economy and, what is more, it was damaging to weak economies of the poor nations. These nations must build their own agriculture and produce their own food to the maximum possible extent, he insisted. For that was the only way they could ever expect to work their way out of hunger and poverty and to raise their own living standards to a tolerable level.

Here again, things have changed quite radically. America's food surplus is much less of a problem today than it was in the fifties and sixties. Its prices have rocketed beyond the reach of poor nations; the surplus is being systematically used to maximize export earnings to narrow the balance of trade deficits; there has even been an atrocious suggestion to use food not "for peace," but "as a weapon"; there is stony reluctance to spare enough tonnage of food to bring relief even to the famine-stricken millions of northeast and central Africa.

And so developing countries are now compelled—mercifully—to fend on their own. Can they do so, how, and how rapidly? These are the questions that should be at the top of the agenda of any discussions relating to the development of the poor nations.

Despite the pervasive gloom and the intimidating dimensions of the world food problem, there is no reason for despair, at least not yet. Though the hour is late, the problem can still be tackled effectively. This confidence is warranted because of two principal reasons: (1) the rich and still unused and underused physical resources of the developing countries—large expanses of arable lands; abundant supply of water despite arid tracts; a warm climate with profuse sunshine ideal for multiple—and where enough water is available, for year-round—cropping; huge manpower which, though a burden, can be turned into an asset; and (2) advanced technologies now available, especially as high-yielding varieties, to bring about a rapid increase in per-acre productivity.

Our best hope today lies in capitalizing on the potential of the high-yielding varieties that have emerged, or are emerging, from the series of international centers that have been established in the last twenty years for crop research in tropical agriculture. Since there has been a good deal of misconception—and much groaning and grumbling—about the Green Revolution, let me try to set the perspective right.

When the dwarf wheat, Norman Borlaug's handiwork, burst upon the scene packed with spectacular yield and began to spread, cutting a wide swath across three continents, some ingenious mind promptly labelled it as a "Green Revolution." The nomenclature had a distinct Madison Avenue ring; "green" in this context meant "not red," and its transparent purpose was to unlock a more liberal supply of aid dollars from a tight-fisted Congress. Whatever the motive, it must be admitted in retrospect that the phrase was unfortunate and has been the source of much confusion. The initial publicity it received was overdone; the expectations it aroused ran too high, and so a reaction was bound to follow. As the world stumbled anew into a food crisis in 1973 and continued to coast along the brink of fresh ones, many questioned the very existence of such a revolution. In their sweeping negativism they overlooked two incontestable facts. First, in the biological sense, there has indeed been a revolution. Genetically improved varieties of wheat, rice, corn, sorghum, pulses, potato, cassava, and other major crops grown in the tropics, including some vegetables, are already there. These "on-the-shelf" and "near-shelf" technologies are capable of raising the average acre-yield several-fold.

And second, but for these new varieties the world food situation today would have been incomparably worse, and "Famine 1975" might well have become a reality. To cite just one example, food-grain production in India rose from 82 million (metric) tons in 1969–1971 to 132 million tons in 1978–1979. During the same period production of wheat more than trebled—from 11 million to 34 million tons; the production of rice, too, rose from 35 million to 54 million tons. These increases were possible mainly because of the high-yielding varieties. But for them India would have found it impossible to feed its soaring population even on the present low level of nutrition. For in the last two decades its population grew from 439 million to 683 million, or by 56 percent.

Some scientists prefer to speak of a "seed-fertilizer revolution," rather than of a "green revolution" which they find colorful, but vague. This has some merit inasmuch as it focuses attention on the two primary ingredients that constitute the heart of the Green Revolution. But it suffers from the fact that its focus is much too narrow, and therefore it misses the vision of the exciting vistas that the high-yielding varieties have opened up for the developing countries.

In fact, what we are experiencing is something far more momentous; the age of science that suddenly burst on the static scene of tropical agriculture. The dwarfs are the harbingers of this new age; and they have brought with them a ringing message of hope. They have already given enough glimpses of a world of plenty that lies within our reach. We stand on the threshold of an all-encompassing *revolution in tropical agriculture*. This is the real meaning of the Green Revolution. Our foremost concern at this stage must be to spread it systematically and as rapidly as we can.

It follows that the frequent reports we hear about its demise are highly exaggerated. More to the point are Bob Dylan's words which, written in a different context, echo through all this cynicism: "It looks like it's a-dyin' an' it's hardly been born."

Yet, in fairness we must admit that the critics of the Green Revolution certainly have some valid points. It has, without doubt, created turmoil in the countryside, led to waves of evictions of tenants and sharecroppers, and has in general made the rich richer and the poor poorer in rural areas. Its progress, too, has slowed down, and in many areas it has already hit a plateau. While all this is true, the underlying reasons are only too often distorted or misunderstood. The fault lies not with the Green Revolution per se, but with the failure to accommodate it properly and to take advantage of its unique potential for the benefit of the masses of people.

Speaking to a Symposium on the Conquest of Hunger held in 1967, Dr. Norman Borlaug argued: National production programs should be organized not for a "slow, steady increase of yields," but for a "revolution in production." When yields are changed from 500 to 5,000 kilos per hectare, "a cataclysmic reaction occurs across the whole spectrum of human activity."

Echoing the same sentiment, others have argued that there was not much a country like India could do by way of boosting production until the arrival of the high-yielding varieties. This is an ex-post-facto whitewash of some grievous defaults of the previous years. A great deal could, and should, have been done even in the days of old, or "traditional," agriculture. This is particularly true of two crucial areas: land reform and road-building.

India, for example, had for decades declared a land-to-the-tiller program as a foremost national goal, but after independence it was virtually bypassed in almost all areas. The country was decolonized, but it was not defeudalized. Absentee landlordism is still rampant, and the farmlands are crowded with tenants-at-will and sharecroppers-at-will. They lack the incentive to work intensively since they cannot retain enough of what they earn with the sweat of their brow. And they cannot obtain credit—to raise crops or to improve their land—since they have no asset they could mortgage as collateral. The landlord, as a rule, flourishes by exploiting not land, but people. And productivity remains abysmally low.

The Green Revolution, in its economic impact and wealth-creating potential, resembles the Industrial Revolution that started in Britain just over two hundred years ago and gradually swept over Western Europe. But in one respect there is a big difference. Whereas the Industrial Revolution arrived *after* the liquidation of the feudal system and the emancipation of the serfs, the Green Revolution exploded overnight right in the heart of a feudal milieu, accompanied by a biomedical revolution and a population explosion. Inevitably it created enormous convulsions. The landlords saw unique opportunities—both in mechanized farming with the new seeds and in soaring land prices—to multiply their wealth rapidly. There followed large-scale resumptions of land and evictions of tenants. The land-to-the-tiller plan was now turned upside down. Is it surprising that in such a situation the rich should get richer, and the poor poorer?

Yet, how different would have been the postwar history if the land reform movement, after setting shining examples of success in Japan, South Korea, and Taiwan, had not been abruptly shelved in the late forties! Though not commonly recognized, it became the first casualty of the Cold War. What emerged next was a de facto alliance between the feudal interests of the developing countries and the so-called aid programs. Even the United Nations family toed the passive line and soft-pedalled the land-reform issue. The biological engineers who had ushered in the dwarfs remained surprisingly reticent about it. What should have been the number one item on any rational agenda for Third-World development was quietly erased from it. We are still paying a staggering penalty for this egregious default.

The Green Revolution, as we all know, is in essence a gene revolution. Its centerpiece is a new plant-type—a dwarf with stiff straw, erect leaves, a strong root system, able to absorb a lot of sunshine and large doses of fertilizers—to give, say, five to six times more yield when properly cultured. And it grows well even when the days are short or the sky is cloudy, and so it matures quickly—in three to four months. It follows that where water supply is assured, we can grow three to four crops a year with these varieties.

The *traditional plant* has been restructured and turned ingeniously into a dwarf to multiply its grain-yielding capability. Our next task, as I emphasized several years ago, was to restructure the *traditional environment* to accommodate the dwarf comfortably so that it could readily yield up its bounties. More specifically I argued: "The tall varieties of wheat and rice had to be dwarfed to produce the seeds of the Green Revolution. The critical dwarfing genes came from Japan and Taiwan. To make the most of the new seeds, big farms, too, will need to be dwarfed. For the right model one can best turn, once again, to the same two sources."[3]

But what about the size of holdings? Those who worry that they might be too small will do well to look at the productivity of farms in Japan, Taiwan, and South Korea, also of the private plots in Soviet Russia and continental China. Indeed, if small is ever beautiful, it should above all be a small, family-owned tropical farm, intensively cultivated for mixed crops and aimed at maximum production, income, and jobs per acre.

The restructuring of the environment has yet another major dimension which, though axiomatic, is only too often overlooked by experts as well as laypeople. Let me use an exaggerated analogy to highlight the point. Suppose the United States had no "Drang nach Westen" (Drive to the New Frontiers), and had remained confined to the Eastern seaboard states which, just over two hundred years ago, joined hands to establish the Federation. How different would have been its history! And what would have happened to its farmlands and its crop production which has become a pillar of its economy and of the world food system!

To a large extent this is the kind of anomaly most developing countries are suffering from today. The colonial masters, for obvious reasons, dropped ports at convenient spots which in due course dotted the coastlines of the three continents they came to dominate. The ports grew into towns, then into cities; more recently, quite a few of them have expanded into sprawling megalopolises; and inevitably they have become the centers of development along with a large infusion of Western culture. The sea-lanes were the umbilical cords that tied them to the metropolitan powers. That pattern has remained largely intact even after decolonization. Or, one might say, without much violence to facts, that the rural areas have become the colonies of *native* rulers. The vast hinterlands have remained isolated. Quite often goods cannot move even short distances of twenty to thirty miles within a country, even though they can travel thousands of miles across the seas.

The seeds of the Green Revolution cannot flourish in rural communities languishing in such total isolation. Even if the seeds somehow manage to reach them, who will cultivate them? Even primitive farmers are not foolish enough to produce surpluses they know they will not be able to move to a market.

Thus, the feudal chains have been reinforced by spatial chains; and the two together spell subsistence farming. This is overwhelmingly the case in most developing countries even today. Their agriculture, it follows, must be liberated from this dual bondage if the Green Revolution is to spread far and wide, instead of being confined to some isolated pockets.

An eminent British agricultural economist, Professor A. W. Ashby, was fond of saying, "If I could do only one thing in a region to spur agricultural development, I would build roads. If to this I could add a second, I would build more roads. And if to these I could add a third, I would build still more roads." This is what we should have done long before the arrival of the high-yielding varieties. Can we afford not to do so even now?

Roads must of course be built in a rational sequence—to keep down costs, to minimize the time lag, and to maximize the pay-off. Obviously, the right places to begin are the densely-populated rural areas. In such areas there are, almost always, primitive—or notional—marketplaces where farmers bring their meager surpluses after laboriously—and wastefully—negotiating dirt roads and no-roads. All-weather village-to-market roads, with a few modern facilities of a market-town provided in these central places, will make an immediate economic impact. They will spur farm production and spawn a host of local industries and services. Adam Smith will then come alive, stimulating exchange of goods and services on an increasing scale.

The objective should of course be to extend these feeder roads in stages, linking the small market-towns to larger townships, to cities, and to the big metropolitan areas, creating a rural-urban continuum which is the backbone of a modern economy.

Land-to-the-tiller, roads with neighborhood market-towns—these are the two prime movers of agriculture, also the most powerful levers of progress, which developing countries most urgently need today. With them even primitive farming can be catapulted into the scientific age surprisingly fast.

A modern science-intensive agriculture will of course need a good many other things to ensure rapid progress, viz., seeds, fertilizers, plant protection; consolidation of holdings; soil conservation; irrigation and water management; research, extension, education; incentive price; credit supply; transportation, warehousing; farmer cooperatives; mixed farming to boost incomes; an effective administrative apparatus; sound, agri-oriented government policies. The list is long and, prima facie, daunting. However, once the two basic prerequisites mentioned above are satisfied, the rest will be greatly facilitated. Indeed, many of the things will tend to fall into place more or less automatically as a result of the internal dynamics of a revitalized rural economy.

Here are some of the time-tested consequences that will ensue. As owners, farmers will take constant care to protect the land and to conserve the soil in order to build up the asset value of their property. Unlike tenants and share-croppers, they should have no difficulty in obtaining the credit they need to raise crops, to purchase equipment and other supplies, to improve their land. They will soon see the advantages of having all their bits and pieces of land in one compact block wherever physically feasible, rather than leave them scattered over a wide area as is now the case. This should produce a groundswell for consolidating the holdings, erasing the crazy-quilt pattern inherited from the past, and radically changing the landscape.

Such consolidation will, in itself, amount to a major revolution. It is also a sine qua non for a rational system of irrigation, and therefore for intensive farming based on multiple cropping. To further boost farm incomes, this may be mixed with cattle-breeding, poultry-raising, pond fishery, and cultivation of a wide range of vegetables and fruits. Each of these categories has large untapped potential to multiply food production and farm incomes. Pond-fish culture offers, to quote FAO, "the most spectacular possibilities of rapid expansion" by increasing both the area under pond culture and yields from existing ponds. This is the remark the agency made in its "Indicative World Plan for Agricultural Development" unveiled in 1970. It is also indicative of the inertia that characterizes the aid programs that so little has been done in the intervening years to activate this potential.

Here are some of the other things we may confidently expect, once agriculture comes to be dominated by owner-farmers. In their own interest, farmers will readily join hands to procure their supplies and to sell their produce on more advantageous terms; genuine cooperatives will mushroom as a result of this grassroots movement. Once farmers own their land, one of the very first things they will do is to build homes, however modest, for themselves, largely using local materials and their own family labor. This will boost housing and building-related industries, create millions of new jobs, and, by satisfying a prime necessity at relatively low cost, raise their living standards.

It is fascinating to reflect on the larger ramifications of these trends. Once the great majority of the tillers in the developing nations are turned into landowning farm families (India alone has 65 million or more such families), they will be fully employed on their farms; the multiplier effects of fast-rising farm productivity will spill over in all directions, creating countless opportunities for new jobs, both on the farm and off the farm. This will, at last, break the back of the massive problem of rural unemployment, put to productive work the billions of idle person-hours that now run to waste, and multiply the rate of GNP growth.

All these trends should set in more or less by themselves. However, progress will be greatly accelerated if concerted action is taken on four other fronts, national and international.

First, all developing countries sorely need comprehensive *rural works programs*—to build roads, market-towns, warehouses, to construct small-to-medium irrigation projects, to conserve soil and water through gulley-plugging, contour-bunding and other measures, to reforest wastelands, to reclaim marshy or waterlogged areas, and to carry out other agri-related activities. Together, they form an integral part of restructuring the environment mentioned earlier. They will provide jobs for the idle and dizzily rising workforce in rural areas. And they will also create strong underpinnings—the sinews—of a modern agriculture.

But how will they be financed? This brings me to the second point, namely, *finance*, the hardy perennial that crops up constantly and is treated as the biggest stumbling block. Yet, formidable as it looks, it is largely our own creation. We predicate development on massive external finance running into billions of dollars, and then throw up our hands in despair because aid on such a scale is not forthcoming! We have long preached the gospel of self-reliance in the developing countries only to make them ever more dependent, at least mentally, on external aid. We have talked of "operation boot-strap," but have trapped them with false hopes. It is time to treat the billions of wasted person-hours as equivalent to billions of dollars and to cash them in aggressively.

India's national leader Mahatma Gandhi used to say, "A man is born not simply with a mouth, but also two hands." Model-building development economists must learn to program this elementary truth into their computers if they are to be worthy of their professional salt. In every developing country there is a vast potential for productive job opportunities. This, in essence, is the mirror image of underdevelopment. Besides, one must remember that some 45 to 50 percent of the population in developing countries is below fifteen years in age. Their fragile economies are groaning under the burden of a huge population of dependent children and teenagers. What could be more irrational—and inhuman—than to saddle them in addition with a huge burden of jobless adults? What we really need is to expand production credit boldly to finance a whole array of high-yielding, quick-maturing projects, and to mobilize the vast human resources to work on them. In fact, all activities relating to the Green Revolution should fully qualify for credit finance. The yield-packed miracle seeds—along with the land, water, and the profuse sunshine of the tropics—should be adequate collateral for even the most conservative bankers of the world.

My third item relates to something that came like a bolt from the blue—the *fertilizer crisis*, which is an offspring of the energy problem. The miracle seeds have been—and are being—evolved on the assumption that fertilizers will be available in abundance and at an affordable price. Then came the overnight quadrupling of the oil price at the end of 1973; and since then there has been a second quadrupling spread over the last few years. Together, they have dealt a heavy blow to the nascent Green Revolution just when it had started to gain momentum. Yet, a way must be found out of the present predicament. A crying need of the hour is to make an all-out effort to vastly step up fertilizer production—to feed the high-yielding varieties flowing out of the international crop research centers so that they may, in turn, feed the surging population of the Third World.

Here is an intriguing thought: Would it be possible to set up a series of fertilizer factories at suitable locations *within the developing countries* as a logical complement to the work of international crop-research centers? The ideal approach would be to establish these fertilizer plants on a *tripartite basis*—with crude oil and capital furnished by the OPEC members; up-to-date technologies, machinery, and managerial knowhow supplied by the Western countries, which will of course include Japan; and local labor and other facilities provided by the host countries. All three will stand to gain tremendously from such joint ventures, and, through such action, they can help conquer hunger and famine once and for all. This is the approach that needs to be energetically explored at the international level today.

Finally, though much progress has been made on the *research front*, a great deal more remains to be done. Wide crosses like those made between wheat and rye may open up new possibilities to produce more food of higher nutritive value at a low unit cost. A spectacular breakthrough, which seems tantalizingly close, would be nitrogen fixation for nonleguminous plants. If and when this comes true, it will liberate agriculture from one more bondage—its dependence on factory-produced nitrogenous fertilizers. Research on the food front must continue with the same relentless vigor as research on the health front. For, it is a kind of "Open Sesame" that can miraculously open up shorter and quicker routes to a future of abundance.

Moreover, health and food are complementary. WHO has drawn up a bold and imaginative program called *Health for All by the Year 2000*. But, clearly, it can succeed only if it moves in lockstep with another program, namely, *Food for All* to be accomplished also in the last stretch of the twentieth century. What good will it do if large segments of humankind are painstakingly rescued from deadly diseases and are delivered to protein-calorie malnutrition, if not to stark hunger?

There is a great deal that international aid-givers and national planners can learn from the World Health Organization and its systematic, goal-conscious, fact-oriented approach in dealing with a major problem like malaria, tuberculosis, bilharziasis, or trypanosomaisis. This is the kind of approach they must apply also in dealing with the four great problems of the Third World: poverty, hunger, population, and illiteracy.

When they get sufficiently serious about tackling the problem of world hunger, they will end their scatter-shot programing, their hit-or-miss methods without sorting out the priorities, and will concentrate their efforts, above all, on the half-dozen crucial items that have been outlined above. When this happens, freedom from hunger will cease to be a dream and a yearning of the soul. It will then be well on its way to becoming a reality.

What, then, is the prognosis? Over the years I have come to consider myself, like René Dubois, a "despairing optimist." At this point, my optimism is warranted by some excellent reasons:

America's food surplus has ceased to be a problem; it has shrunken in size, its function has changed, and its price has soared too high for most developing nations. They can no longer fool themselves with the thought that America can, or will, feed their teeming millions.

The aid dollars—that is, dollars available for nonmilitary aid—are dwindling fast. In Washington, the budget axe is falling mercilessly even on essential social programs amidst cries of agony. This is hastening a chastening process among Third World nations. They cannot much longer chase the will-o'-the-wisp of massive transfer of resources from the affluent countries.

The petrodollar hordes piled up by the OPEC nations have flooded the "North" for several years almost to the point of saturation. They are now slowly turning "Southward" in one form or another.

The rich nations know more than ever before that to run their industrial machine they need secure supplies of raw materials, especially a number of key minerals, from the poor nations; that they can no longer commandeer them and can obtain them only through fair deals on a give-and-take basis. Besides, caught in a zero-sum growth in world trade, they are bickering bitterly among themselves for limited markets. As a result, they are waking up to the realization that the pie of world trade can be greatly enlarged by speeding economic growth and spreading prosperity in the South.

Finally, there is a heartening signal—of all places from turbulent El Salvador. The middle-of-the-road moderates, in a frantic eleventh-hour move to avert the worst, pushed through a radical land-to-the-tiller program. Though it has been caught in a crossfire between the ultra-rightists and the ultra-leftists, it has apparently gained solid support from the army of newly-created owner-farmers. The Reagan regime, too, after its precipitate plunge, is having second and third thoughts. And it may yet veer round to the realistic conclusion that its best bet to avoid another Vietnam in El Salvador, and to bring peace and stability to this troubled land, is to lend full support to the land reform to make it an unalloyed success.

El Salvador, however, is only a curtain-raiser. The struggle that has begun here to "win the hearts and minds of the people," to use a Vietnam-era phrase, with equitable land distribution among the actual tillers as the central issue in this relentless tug of war, is destined to spread to other countries. Ironically, we are coming full circle to realizing once again, after three decades of groping in the wilderness, that land-to-the-tiller programs have a most vital role to play, that this is the only road that can lead to rapid economic growth along with social justice, and therefore also to peace and stability.

Thus, driven by circumstances, developing countries have begun to move in the right direction, still slowly and clumsily, in reverse gear out of dead ends. But they are at last in sight of the highway. It may be presumed that before long they will muster enough sense to make an about-turn, to get on to the good road, and to move confidently toward the long-cherished goal with all deliberate speed.

Let us hope this will happen soon. There isn't much time left for waste. The clock of global famine is still ticking remorselessly.

NOTES

1. William and Paul Paddock, *Famine 1975! America's Decision: Who Will Survive?* (Boston: Little, Brown, 1967); *Time of Famine: America and the Food Crisis, a New Edition of Famine 1975!* (Boston: Little, Brown, 1976).

2. Reported in *The New York Times*, November 24, 1975. Emphasis added.

3. Sudhir Sen, *A Richer Harvest: New Horizons for Developing Countries* (Maryknoll, N.Y.: Orbis Books, and New Delhi: Tata McGraw-Hill, 1974), p. 301. See also *Reaping the Green Revolution* (Maryknoll, N.Y.: Orbis Books, and New Delhi: Tata McGraw-Hill, 1975).

9

INCREASING AVAILABILITY OF FOOD
FOR THE WORLD'S POOR

D. Gale Johnson

Two critical assumptions have determined the general approach of this essay. The two assumptions are, first, the primary source of malnutrition or undernutrition is poverty, and, second, the majority of the world's poor people live in rural areas and not in cities. The first assumption carries with it the implication that lack of food is not the source of malnutrition in most instances but the existence and persistence of mild to serious malnutrition is primarily due to insufficient purchasing power. The second assumption means that there are direct links between increasing productivity of agricultural resources and the incomes of farm people on the one hand, and the production of food on the other hand. One of the important means of reducing poverty in farm areas is to increase the productivity of land and labor; the increased productivity will be reflected in the increased production of food.

The poor people of the world are primarily rural and farm residents. The World Bank has estimated that 80 percent of the world's poor live in rural areas. One does not find most of a nation's poor people in the teeming masses of Calcutta or the slums of Mexico City, but in rural and farm areas. That we have a different impression is due to the fact that in urban areas the poor are exposed to casual observation while most of us are not so distressed by the rural poor, if for no other reason than that one sees relatively few of them at a given time. And most visitors to the low-income countries spend much more time in the cities than in rural areas where the poverty is even greater but much less visible.

The fact that the majority of the world's poor live in rural areas has important implications to the relative roles of increasing productivity and food production, on the one hand, and of increasing the food available to the poorest of the poor through a more equal distribution of the available food supplies. Very few countries have the administrative capacity or the rural infrastructure to achieve significant modifications in the distribution of the

D. Gale Johnson is professor of economics, University of Chicago.

available food supplies in rural areas. Even in those instances where food price subsidies have been extended to rural areas there has often been an adverse effect upon the incentives to produce food. But perhaps the most important point is that, when external aid is provided to pay for the food distribution schemes, the resources that poor countries devote to food subsidies could be used for investment in both human and physical capital.

I am moderately optimistic that the poor people of the world will be better fed in 1990 than in 1980 and in 2000 than in 1990. That optimism is based upon the trends of the past several decades and the known potentials that exist for the improvement of food supply and nutrition and increases in income opportunities in farm and rural areas. While one can give examples of urban people having improved their incomes and opportunities while rural people gained little, I know of no examples of the opposite during this century. Improvements in the circumstances of rural and farm people have uniformly contributed to the growth and prosperity of urban areas. Fortunately for farm people, most of the time they have participated in the growth of real incomes that have benefited the urban populations, though often with considerable time lags. The underlying factors—improvements in human and physical capital, changes in technology, and the growth and extension of markets—cannot indefinitely be monopolized for the benefit of the urban areas but must eventually be shared with rural areas.

WHAT WE CAN LEARN FROM HISTORY

A source of my cautious optimism that the poor people of the world will be better nourished in the future than at present is the trends for the period since the end of World War II. I shall indicate what some of the major trends have been by asking five questions. It is probable that the majority of you who read this would believe the answers were in the affirmative for perhaps as many as three of them:

Is a larger percentage of the world's population subject to famine today than at the beginning of this century?

Do hundreds of millions fail to get enough to eat every day of their lives?

Has the growth of population in the low-income countries outpaced the growth of food production?

Has the gap in life expectancy between the developing and industrial countries been increasing over time?

Has infant mortality increased in the developing countries as the result of the introduction of milk substitutes by the multinational food companies?

The answer to each question is negative and there is documented evidence to support that answer in each case. Yet if your only information comes from the major transmitters of print and electronic information you would not be so far wrong in believing that you should accept an affirmative answer to most of the questions. The Presidential Commission on World Hunger was responsible for the repetition of an incorrect statement, later retracted by its source, that a large percentage of the world's population goes to bed hungry every night. Even if it were true that many people do not get enough to eat every day, no one who understands rural life in the developing countries believes that hunger would not be relieved during harvest time for food crops or the slaughter of an animal. In fact, the authors of an abridged version of the Commission's report modified the bald statement to read "One out of every eight people on earth is hungry most of the time." Even that statement is more false than true.

Famine afflicts far fewer people today than it did a century ago. This is true in an absolute sense, not just in a relative sense. Thus even though the world's population has increased threefold in a century, far fewer people are afflicted with famine today than a century ago. The Presidential Commission noted that the incidence of famine has been greatly diminished: ". . . widespread starvation due to natural causes has been relatively rare during the past 35 years, thanks to improved national and international capabilities for mobilizing emergency assistance in time of need." The Commission notes, quite correctly, that "Food shortages and famine caused by political conflict have proved harder to overcome." Reference is made to the Nigerian Civil War of 1967–1970, the Indo-Pakistani conflict of 1971–1972, and the more recent tragic events in Cambodia and Nicaragua. It is then noted that as "tragic and newsworthy as these events are," the world's major food problem is not famine or starvation "but the less dramatic one of chronic malnutrition." I agree with this conclusion.

But I find it difficult to understand why the Commission did not pause for at least a moment to note that the twentieth century had come very close to the elimination of one of the greatest scourges of the poor people of the world, namely famine resulting from crop failure or other natural causes. This is an achievement of greatest moment, equal in significance to almost any improvement in the human condition that one can imagine. It is something to which the people of this century should point to with pride, and justifiably so, though only a tiny percentage of us realize that something of such great benefit to the world's poor has occurred.

In the low-income or developing countries, per capita food production has increased in each of the last three decades at a modest rate, perhaps at an annual rate of 0.5 percent. The increase has not been uniform. While there have been increases in per capita food production in both Asia and Latin America, the past two decades have seen significant declines in per capita food production in most of Africa. During the 1970s per capita food production fell by 15 percent, an outcome that one could hardly imagine if it had not occurred.

Between 1950 and 1978 life expectancy at birth in the low-income developing countries (those with per capita incomes in 1978 of $360 or less) increased
from thirty-five years to fifty years and the gap between these countries and
the industrial countries decreased from thirty-one to twenty-four years. The
present state of life expectancy in the world's poorest countries may be put in
perspective by noting that the United States did not achieve a life expectancy
of fifty years until 1910 and Japan did not reach it until the late 1940s.

Reductions in child and infant mortality have been responsible for a significant percentage of the increase in life expectancy as well as for the rapid
growth in population in the low-income countries. However, as I will emphasize later, the reduction in infant and child mortality is being followed by
significant reductions in birth rates in most of the low-income countries. The
rapid population growth rates since World War II in the developing countries
have had some noticeable negative effects through straining the capacities of
the economics to provide a sufficiency of almost everything to meet the rapidly growing demand—housing, schools, sewers, water, streets, roads, and
food. But we should never emphasize solely the negative side of the type of
rapid population growth the world has witnessed during the past three decades. The reduction in human suffering and pain that has accompanied the
sharp decline in infant and child mortality has been of enormous benefit to
hundreds of millions.

THINGS THAT HAPPENED IN THE 1970s
AND SOME THAT DIDN'T

The 1970s began full of hope for the rapid expansion of food production in
the low-income countries. The Green Revolution had spread at a rapid pace
across South Asia and in Mexico and was showing promise in North Africa
and the Middle East. World grain stocks were increasing owing, at least in
part, to the reduction in demand for grain imports in the developing countries. Grain prices in international markets after adjustment for inflation
were below the prices of the Great Depression of the thirties. Some who had
been so sure in the early and mid-1960s that the poor countries had lost the
capacity to feed themselves would pronounce during the late 1960s that the
Green Revolution had been so successful that "the world has recently entered
a new agricultural era." The "sweeping advances in food production in
several major developing countries" were dated by saying "the old era ended
in 1966 and the new era began in 1967." Neither the excessive pessimism of
the early and mid-1960s or the undue optimism of the late 1960s was justified.

The major exporters responded to low grain prices by cutting back production of grain, especially of wheat. As a consequence grain stocks were reduced and when there was a modest shortfall in world grain production in
1972, grain prices increased sharply. Once again the prophets of doom came
forward to proclaim that the world's poor people faced a permanent decline
in their wellbeing as a result of a long-run shortfall in the rate of growth of
food production and a sharp rise in the cost of food. Some argued that the

cost of food was to rise in the years ahead because of the adverse effects of higher energy prices, working through fertilizer prices, upon the ability to expand food production, because the world's supply of arable land had been exhausted, and the rising appetite for meat in high-income countries was causing grain to be diverted from food for people to feed for animals.

Briefly, since fertilizer technology has changed and energy is but one (albeit an important) component in producing fertilizer, the prices paid by farmers for fertilizer in March 1981 relative to prices paid for all purchased production inputs were more than 10 percent below the late 1960s and a quarter below 1975 prices. Similar price patterns exist in the low-income countries that relate their fertilizer prices to international market prices. During the most recent decade for which data are available, the amount of arable land in the developing market economies increased by 8 percent. But, more importantly, the irrigated area in the low-income countries increased by 25 percent or approximately 20 million hectares. Finally, grain used as feed by the developed market economies of North America and Europe is now approximately the same as during 1972/73. The increase in world grain use as feed has all occurred in the centrally planned economies and the developing market economies themselves. The percentage of the world's grain fed to livestock is now slightly smaller than during the early 1970s.

A World Food Conference was held in 1974. At that time the fear was expressed that the major grain and food exporters could not expand their exports enough to meet the requirements of the developing countries, especially the heavily populated countries of South Asia. At the time there remained optimism concerning the performance of agriculture in the centrally planned economies. China was to continue to be a modest net exporter of grains and the other centrally planned economies were to stabilize their imports at the low level of the late 1960s and early 1970s. Something odd occurred. During the 1970s world grain exports grew at an unprecedented rate, increasing by 90 percent. South Asia will import little more than a million tons of grain in the current year out of world grain exports of more than 200 million tons. During two recent years India actually exported a small amount of grain, including some to the USSR as well as to Vietnam. The centrally planned economies accounted for 55 percent of the increase in world grain exports during the 1970s, with the Soviet Union now having the honor of being the world's largest grain importer and China in third place behind Japan.

Developing countries have increased their grain and other food imports substantially. But relatively little of the increase has come in the low-income developing countries—those with less that $360 per capita income in 1978 dollars. The increases have occurred in the middle-income developing countries, such as South Korea, Mexico, Brazil, and the OPEC countries. The increased imports of the middle-income developing countries are not an indication of failure of their agricultures; instead the higher levels of import result from their success in achieving a high rate of growth with its consequent effects upon the demand for food.

PROSPECTS FOR THE 1980s

As I have noted, per capita food production in the developing countries increased during the past three decades. The improvement was modest over all, and in much of Africa per capita food production declined. There is no reason to anticipate that the 1980s will show less improvement in per capita food consumption in the low-income countries than has been achieved during the past two or three decades. The potential for greater improvement clearly exists, though a cautious and realistic view is that during the 1980s, as during the previous two decades, performance will fall short of potential. However, as I shall note later, there are some positive factors that may result in a higher growth rate of per capita food consumption and production in the low-income countries during the 1980s than during the 1970s and 1960s.

While I shall give considerable emphasis in the following pages to the potentials for increasing agricultural and food production in the low-income countries, I want it to be understood that I approach such growth as much from the point of view of increasing agricultural productivity and incomes as I do in terms of the increases in food supply. Fundamentally, the cause of malnutrition and food insufficiency in the world and in the low-income countries is poverty and not the lack of availablility of food. It is basically true that anyone who has sufficient income has no lack of food. Given that we now have a world food system, with almost all of the world's more than 4 billion people with potential access to food wherever it may have been produced, only lack of income or governmental intervention are sufficient causes for hunger and malnutrition. And in rural areas the primary source of income is the productivity of the land and labor used to produce agricultural products. Consequently increasing agricultural productivity serves both to increase incomes and to provide the additional food, either directly or through trade, to meet the greater demand due to the higher incomes.

THE GREEN REVOLUTION

For many people a look ahead at what the 1980s hold for incomes and food supplies in the low-income countries is influenced by their answer to the question: "What happened to the Green Revolution?" Asking this question generally implies that the benefits of research underlying the development of the new grain varieties and the cultural practices that were called the Green Revolution were less than anticipated. One reason the question is asked was the unfortunate designation of the new high-yielding varieties of rice and wheat as miracle varieties. The use of the term Green Revolution also held out the hope of major, yes, revolutionary changes in food supplies. The new varieties represented remarkable achievements, but one thing must be learned about research and agriculture—a single revolution is never enough. What is required is a stream of revolutions, each perhaps with rather modest effect but with significant cumulative influence.

While the new high-yielding varieties had a more modest effect on production than their most avid supporters hoped for, the availability of the new varieties indicated how responsive the poor and often illiterate farmers of the developing countries are when new and more profitable opportunities are made available. In India, for example, by 1976/77, 35 percent of all rice and more than 70 percent of all wheat were sown with the new varieties. The doubling of wheat yields and the trebling of wheat output in India would have been impossible without the new wheat varieties.

GRAIN YIELD TRENDS

The emphasis upon grain when we talk about the developments and prospects for the low-income countries is due to the great importance of grain as the source of income for farm people and the large percentage of calories that comes from grain. In the low-income developing countries approximately 70 percent of all calories come from grain. Thus anything that favorably affects the production of grain, as did the Green Revolution in the areas that could adopt the new varieties, has the potential for improving both incomes and nutrition. The 1970s saw repeated references to the possibility, if not the probability, that the growth rate of grain yields was declining in the world. The feeling of unease was buttressed for many by grain yields in the United States, especially corn, in 1975 and 1976 and, to a lesser degree, in 1977, that were below prior peak yield levels. Thus some concluded that grain yields in the United States were slowing down and may even have reached their peak levels. From this view it was not too difficult to conclude that the experience of the U.S. would be followed by similar adverse trends in the rest of the world.

However, corn yields in the United States in 1979 set a new record and even the average of 1979 and 1980, in spite of the 1980 drought in much of the Corn Belt, was above the trend level of corn yields for the United States. There has been a tendency to assume that most, if not all, of the benefits of the Green Revolution were obtained in the first few years and with the then record crops in the developing countries in 1969–1971. During the 1960s the annual average grain-yield increase in the developing market economies was 1.8 percent; in the 1970s the annual increase was the same. For the world the increase in grain yields did decline, from 2.8 percent annually in the 1960s to 1.7 percent in the 1970s. The decline in grain yields did not presage an increase in grain prices; in real terms international grain prices were as low or lower in the late 1970s as during the 1960s. But the important point I wish to make is that in the developing market economies grain yields continued to increase at the same pace in the 1970s as in the 1960s.

I shall now present several reasons to support a degree of optimism for improvement in the circumstances of the world's poor people during the remainder of the twentieth century. My emphasis will first be upon changes that can result in improving productivity and income in the rural areas. My remarks must be quite condensed and, to some degree, illustrative. But the points indicate that change has occurred and is occurring.

AGRICULTURAL RESEARCH

During the past two decades there has been a major growth in the expenditures on agricultural research on the farm production problems of the low-income countries. In the fifteen years between 1959 and 1974, agricultural research in the major developing countries (Latin America, Africa, and Asia) increased from $228 million to $957 million (1971 constant dollars). This increase in expenditures occurred both in the international agricultural research centers and in the research institutions of the low-income countries. As a share of an increasing world expenditure on agricultural research, the expenditures in the three low-income regions increased from 17 percent in 1959 to 25 percent in 1974. Since there is a lag of five to ten years between research and actual application on farms, most of the effects of the increased research investments made after 1973 have still not been felt.

IRRIGATION

Earlier it was noted that during the 1970s the irrigated area in the low-income countries increased substantially. Much of the increase in irrigation has occurred in the densely populated regions of the world, principally Asia. Current rates of investment in irrigation in South and Southeast Asia are high by historical standards. Improvement of the irrigation systems is very important in the rice growing areas, since a major factor limiting the spread of the high-yielding varieties of rice has been inadequate control of water depths in existing irrigation systems. The new rice varieties are short and thus an uncontrolled influx of water that covers the plants for a brief period of time results in loss of most of the crop.

INCOME GROWTH

Per capita incomes have been growing in the developing countries and will continue to grow. The World Bank projects an annual rate of per capita income growth for the low-income developing countries (less that $360 per capita income in 1978) of between 2.1 and 2.5 percent, while the middle-income developing countries are projected to grow at about 3 percent. These projections are for oil-importing countries.

If per capita incomes grow at an annual rate of 2.25 percent, in a decade the increase will be 25 percent. For the low-income countries this will mean that the demand for food will increase by approximately half that. If the growth is reasonably well distributed among all segments of the population, the growth in demand will go a substantial distance toward reducing both severe and moderate malnutrition in the lower-income countries.

While we are and should be concerned about the low per capita income levels that still prevail in Asia, especially in the most populous countries, we should not forget that there have been a very considerable number of success stories since World War II. Several of what we now define as middle-income developing countries were clearly low-income developing countries just two decades ago. South Korea, which had a per capita income of $1,160 in 1978, had an income in 1960 that would have classified it as low income by today's criterion. Taiwan would have been at the low end of the middle-income developing countries in 1960, but by 1978 had a per capita income of $1,400; and a life expectancy of seventy-two years, almost identical to ours. While not with such spectacular growth rates, Thailand, the Philippines, and Liberia have moved out of the low-income group during the past two decades. And we should not forget that in 1950 Japan had a per capita gross national product (in 1980 dollars) the same as South Korea's in 1978 and a life expectancy of fifty-six years. While Japan's growth rate has been unusually high, it has been approximately equaled by Hong Kong, Singapore, and South Korea since 1960.

There are more than a billion people in the low-income developing countries. Their per capita gross national product was $245 in 1980. This seems to us to be a pitifully low income, but it is 40 percent greater than in 1960. Over those two decades per capita food intake has increased by 10 percent, life expectancy by about a decade, and the percentage of the population that is literate increased from 29 percent in 1960 to 38 percent in 1975. These changes indicate that substantial improvement have occurred.

SLOWER POPULATION GROWTH

One of the most encouraging signs pointing to further improvement in the circumstances of the world's poor people is the decline in birth rates that has occurred in low-income countries with total populations in excess of two billion. In these countries birth rates declined by more than 15 percent between 1960 and 1977. Several countries had declines of 35 percent or more: Colombia, South Korea, Tunisia, Chile, Taiwan, Costa Rica, Hong Kong, Singapore, Trinidad and Tabago, and China. India had a decline of nearly a fifth.

A slowing down of population growth has two effects upon per capita income and food supply—a larger fraction of the population is in the working ages during the transition period to a lower rate of population growth and there are fewer people eating out of a given food supply or dependent upon the economy's natural resources and capital. These effects will not be large during the 1980s since it is projected that for the decade the annual population growth rate in the low-income developing economies will be 2.1 percent compared to 2.3 percent for the 1970s. Population growth rates are not responding more promptly to the significant decline in birth rates because death rates are declining nearly as rapidly as birth rates. This is not something to bemoan but something about which to rejoice. But as life expectancy approaches sixty years, further reductions in death rates will come much more slowly and the continuing decline in birth rates will be reflected in a substantial reduction in the rate of population growth. If the expected pattern of further rapid declines in birth rates and a slow decline in death rates materializes, then we can anticipate by 2000 population growth rates in the low-income developing countries of well under 1.5 percent.

RURAL-URBAN TENSIONS

In most developing countries, especially during the first two decades after World War II, it was anticipated that surplus agricultural income could be used to finance urbanization. In numerous developing countries a variety of measures were used to extract resources from agriculture and transfer these resources to the urban areas. The methods used included export taxes on agricultural products, low procurement prices for certain food products, restraints on imports of farm inputs that resulted in protection of inefficient domestic industries, and overvalued currencies that inhibited agricultural exports and resulted in low domestic prices for farm products compared to urban products.

The food scare of the early 1970s does seem to have had some effect upon policies in many developing countries. While not all countries responded positively, a number of countries have improved the terms of trade between the farm and the city in recent years. Unfortunately there remains much to be done and even when positive changes are made there is often a justifiable lack of confidence that the changes will be more than transitory.

MORE EQUITABLE DISTRIBUTION OF FOOD AND INCOME

I have so far said little about the possibility of reducing malnutrition by more equal distribution of food or income. I have noted that the primary cause of malnutrition or inadequate food consumption is poverty, not a lack of available food to be purchased. If poverty is the primary reason for malnutrition, would not making the distribution of income more equitable be an appropriate means for reducing malnutrition? Or, put another way, why can't most malnutrition be eliminated by a more equitable distribution of the available supplies of food?

The answer to the first question is probably in the negative; we do not know how to make the distribution of income more equal in the developing countries without serious negative effects upon the growth of real per capita income and productivity. If a country is successful in achieving a more equal distribution of income than would result from the process of economic growth, it is likely to find that such equality has been bought at the expense of increased average incomes and higher incomes for the poor themselves. To argue that an aid proposal must primarily benefit the poorest of the poor means in most cases that it will have little or no effect upon the productivity and long-run earning capacities of those it is designed to help.

It is possible, to a limited degree, to achieve a more equitable distribution of food than would result from usual market forces. This can be done by targeting special groups that will have access to food at less than market prices. The distribution can occur through fair price shops, school lunches, or special programs for mothers and children. The general food-price subsidies on which so many resources are devoted in the centrally planned economies and some market developing economies, such as Egypt, generally fail to equalize food consumption and constitute a substantial impediment to the effective use of resources. Such general food subsidies primarily benefit urban areas. People who live in urban areas have higher average incomes than do farm and other rural people. The existence of costly general food price subsidies often result in the unwillingness of governments to permit farm prices to be at levels that encourage expansion of production since an increase in farm prices constitutes a claim upon governmental revenue.

Given time it is possible to modify the distribution of income to increase both the absolute and relative income of the poor. In fact, the documented experience of nations is that as per capita incomes increase personal incomes become more equal. Some policies and programs may be effective in increasing the rate at which incomes become more equal. The policies that can have this effect are those that increase the human capital available to the poorest segments of the population. But these policies will not have much effect in the short run; the consequences will be evident only over decades. But such effects will be permanent and not transitory or dependent upon aid from outside the community.

CONCLUSION

There are a number of topics that I have not commented upon; some of the exclusions have been due to space limitations but others have been deliberate. I have said very little about the potential effects of natural resource limitations. This is one of the deliberate exclusions. Other than noting that fertilizer prices have not increased in spite of a sharp increase in energy costs or that the world has not yet run out of arable land, I have neglected what many believe to be the most important restraint upon improving the lot of the world's poor, or the rest of us for that matter.

It is my view that natural resources, their lack or abundance, have a relatively minor role in the determination of the wealth of nations. Countries that have had an abundance of resources, such as Argentina, Uruguay, and Brazil, have much lower incomes than other countries with very limited resources, such as Japan, the Netherlands, and Switzerland. Let us not forget that Japan was a relatively poor nation before World War II and even poorer thereafter and yet has emerged with one of the largest economies and nearly the highest per capita income in the world. The gross national product of Japan is nearly as large as that of the Soviet Union, with less than half of the population and but a tiny fraction of the natural resources. Hong Kong and

Singapore are tiny island communities with few natural resources, yet they have joined the industrial nations of the world in little more than three decades.

But for some of you these comparative statements of the irrelevance of natural resource endowments do not speak to the question of worldwide resource limitations. It is true that countries can become rich, as have Japan, Singapore, and Hong Kong to name some recent examples, by manufacturing based on resources from the rest of the world. In other words, a few can generate high incomes by utilizing a large share of the world's flow of natural resources, but this option is not available to all. Or so some claim. But to accept this claim is to assume that human beings have neither the will nor intelligence to seek further improvements in knowledge that will permit finding alternatives to any of the natural resources that have increasing real prices or costs. We are never, ever, going to completely run out of any natural resource; at worst, we will see rising costs of obtaining some resources. At best, we will anticipate changes in real costs of natural resources or of human skills and capacities and make the necessary investments in research and education to either change supplies or to find acceptable alternatives at reasonable cost.

It is relatively easy to be pessimistic about the future of the poor people of the world. But the evidence to support such a view is with little analytical support. And I will conclude with an *obiter dictum*: Whether the incomes and nutrition of the poor people of the world continue to improve will depend primarily upon human beings and not on nature. The vagaries of climate, the available quantities of oil, coal, or uranium, or the amount of agricultural land will not determine the outcome. If the research is undertaken, if policies are adopted that provide reasonable incentives for farmers and other rural people, provide them access to necessary supplies at reasonable prices, and permit products to be sold at the best possible prices, the incomes of the world's poorest people will grow and malnutrition will be largely eliminated.

10

FAMINE AND ECONOMIC DEVELOPMENT

Harvey Leibenstein

In the popular view famines are caused by shortages of food. However, several writers on the subject have taken issue with this view, and have argued that it is not the food shortages per se but the conditions in which people find themselves that determine famines. It is of some importance to examine this problem, since we are concerned with the question as to whether or not economic development as such can reduce or eliminate famines. In other words, if there is a multiplicity of causes, are any of the possible causes changed by economic development to various degrees? At the same time we want to consider the extent to which famines may be viewed as elements which in some sense or other retard economic development.

In my original plan for this essay, I did not expect to be concerned with the causes of famine but only with the consequences of famine and the relation of famine to economic development. However, after considering this question carefully, it seems that a discussion of the causes of famine cannot be avoided. The reason for this is that part of the essay will be concerned about why economic development tends to eliminate famines. This is of necessity related to the probability that development eliminates the causes of famine.

My interest is not with controversy about causes; rather, I am primarily concerned with minimizing controversy and at the same time considering possible causes. In this case, it may be useful to consider three elements which are likely features of the causation of most famines: (1) food shortages, (2) entitlement problems, and (3) vulnerability problems. These elements are likely to be closely interrelated, although in most particular instances some causation elements are likely to predominate. In the pages that follow we will consider each of these elements separately, simply to distinguish various features when we examine the consequences of development on famines, and vice versa.

Harvey Leibenstein is Andelot Professor of Economics and Population, Harvard University.

FOOD SHORTAGES VS. ENTITLEMENT PROBLEMS

Probably the most famous famine (at least to Western readers) is the one involved in the biblical story of Joseph and his brothers. This is a clear case of a cyclic famine in which there are seven years of plenty and seven years of famine. The biblical solution is to have a grain storage system so that the years of plenty operate as a buffer to the years of scarcity. From this point of view, famine can be viewed as being caused by a lack of planning for an essentially cyclic industry. We have cyclic yields over time, and we have to even out availability. However, if famines are not caused essentially by food shortages, then this view of the matter cannot be adequately handled. In addition, we should keep in mind that we need not concentrate only on insurance schemes over time. It is possible to work out related schemes over space. In other words, we can have those countries producing surplus absorb the shocks for others who suffer temporary scarcity and who will repay when these scarcities are eliminated. Thus, on the whole, we can visualize the basic food-shortage problem as essentially one of lack of provision of insurance against risk. There may, of course, be political or other reasons for the lack of insurance at the time it takes place.

The alternative view has been stated forcefully in several articles by Amartya Sen.[1] Sen's argument essentially says that people starve in the midst of plenty because they lack what he refers to as "entitlements." By entitlement we have in mind the various sources of obtaining the means to purchase food. This may be a lack of resources (that is, assets) which could either be sold to obtain funds for purchases, or which could be used as collateral for borrowings in order to purchase food. The other is the lack of current income, from any source, with which to purchase food. The income lack may be a consequence of either unemployment, or crop failure on one's farm or on the farm one works under sharecropping arrangements, or because one works as an independent artisan whose services are not needed because of general depressed conditions in the countryside. In any event, it is the lack of ability of any kind to raise the necessary entitlement that is the source of the problem.

Sen examines four general famines of which the most striking in recent history are the Bengal famine of the 1940s and the famine in Ethiopia in the early seventies. Especially striking is the view of the Ethiopian famine during which the famine took place in villages astride a major highway over which food was simultaneously being shipped to the capital city. Sen argues, especially in the last case, that food as such was not the problem. Clearly here the solution could be found if in some way or other there was a method of giving people "entitlements" which would avoid such famines. Whether such entitlements involve a redistribution of income or not can be examined in some detail. It is possible to think of entitlement schemes which need not involve such income redistribution.

That famines may be caused by food shortages would seem obvious to most readers. That famines may exist without food shortages may appear to be surprising to some. But it is necessary at this point to distinguish food-shortage famines versus entitlement famines. A reasonable criterion of distinguishing the two that could be proposed is: if a famine is of such a nature that no redistribution or rationing of food would eliminate the famine, then this would be viewed as a pure food-shortage famine. For instance, the famine that existed during the siege of Leningrad (1941–1942) was essentially a food-shortage famine. During the siege food was reaching the city in very limited amounts, and a very strict system of rationing was unable to provide more than 900-1,200 (approx.) calories per person. Here entitlement was not the issue. Everyone was issued ration cards. Whatever the causes of the food shortage, it is clear that with respect to Leningrad a clear-cut *shortage* existed. The food shortage was a sufficient cause of famine conditions.

A very striking example of an entitlement famine is that reported by Sen in his description of the famine in Ethiopia, which we mentioned earlier. According to Sen there were a number of famine villages situated along a recently built major highway going to Addis Ababa. During the famine, food was flowing along the highway close to the village area towards the capital city. There is even the implication that some of the food may have been coming from areas close to the famine villages. Clearly the critical factor was not food availability, but the fact that people in the capital city had entitlements whereas those in the famine villages had inadequate entitlements.

The case of what was probably *mostly* an entitlement famine may be said to have existed in Bangladesh in 1974. Here per capita food availability actually increased. Per capita food grains availability rose from 14.9 oz. in 1971 to 15.9 oz. in 1974. In fact, in only about a third of the time between 1961 and 1970 was food availability per capita higher. The famine was caused because there was a reasonable proportion of the population who, for one reason or another, did not have the purchasing power to obtain the food that, in fact, was available somewhere within the country. Strict rationing might have eliminated the famine, but such rationing was not carried out, although some rationing (about 40 percent of food availability) was in force.[2]

A very simple definition of entitlement would be general purchasing power. Put simply, it would refer to the availability of money to purchase goods. Such a definition is much too limited for the kind of analysis we ought to be interested in. Thus, by entitlement we will mean any capacity of an individual to command goods in some way but without the use of force. We assume that most of the ways would be through exchange. Thus, the existence of wealth in any form would involve entitlement, since the components of wealth could be sold for purchasing power. In addition, even in the absence of wealth there may be the possibility of obtaining credit, based on the hope that future earnings may enable the borrower to repay. Of course, there may not be any lenders on this basis. But nonmonetary claims to food must also be taken into account. Thus, those who have family connections to those with purchasing power may also be said indirectly to have entitlements. For example, children rarely have purchasing power in their own right but through their parents or other family members have indirect entitlements. The same may also be true of adults within an extended family system.

There are, of course, situations where money itself is not a sufficient entitlement. This is true wherever some system of rationing occurs; and, hence, the right to a ration card in addition to money (sometimes without money) is necessary in order to be able to obtain or purchase food. In various ways we may consider entitlements to exist from the most direct form, i.e., cash, to a variety of more remote entitlement possibilities. Thus, in a sense, we may view every individual as possessing a direct *and* remote entitlement potential; and, during the course of food shortages, these individuals will gradually run out first of their more direct forms, and gradually out of their more remote entitlement possibilities.

The logic of the entitlement problem as a cause of famine may be seen on the basis of the following made-up example. Consider the case of a gambling casino and observe how it operates. We would note that a high proportion of those who frequent the casino use chips and are gambling at the various tables. On the other hand, there are others who are simply watching without gambling. A survey would reveal that many of those watching had gambled earlier, and would like to continue gambling but they have no chips. Looking at this problem purely from above without knowing any of the internal facts, it may appear that the reason some cannot indulge in the activity is a scarcity of gambling chips. A superficial remedy would be to call some other casino and have them ship in 20 percent more chips in order to provide for the "chips famine" so to speak. But since we understand the workings of the casino, we know that the shipping of more chips is quite irrelevant to the problem—indeed it has nothing to do with it. Having twice as many chips will not change the fact that a proportion of the casino inhabitants do not have sufficient funds to purchase additional chips. What appears like a chips famine cannot in fact be altered or relieved by adding chips. While this example is extreme and artificial, nevertheless it does indicate the logic of the entitlement problem. It helps us to see that in some cases adequate food supplies can be associated with famine, and furthermore that merely shipping food supplies may not necessarily help.

It is of interest to note that a pure entitlement approach may also be misleading. To continue with the gambling-casino analogy, offering a given amount of credit per gambler does not necessarily help. Some would simply play for proportionately higher stakes and lose just as rapidly. Some would get somewhat longer runs at the table. But a proportion would not play because they had lost at the tables earlier. Similarly, it may be true that the lack of ability to purchase food may appear to be the cause of famine. Nevertheless, there are certainly instances where the entitlement difficulty is itself caused by a change in food-supply conditions. In most areas where famine occurs, the basic activity of most people is agriculture or activities closely related to agriculture. Thus, some element connected with food supply may change entitlement *availability* even if the surface reason appears to be an entitlement problem. Two possibilities come to mind. First, those whose incomes are directly derived from agriculture may find that their incomes disappear as a result of some adversity related to agriculture. Various examples which come to mind are bad harvests, crop blight and disease, some form of commercial crop failure so that a change in prices may mean that inputs cost more than output is worth, a lack of rainfall or other adversities dealing with water supply, a shift of the salt level of the water table so that previously fertile land becomes infertile, and so on. Second, we have to consider the laborers and artisans in agricultural areas who themselves are not involved in the growing of food, but whose income is derived from the expenditures of those who do grow food. Hence, if in the first instance agricultural supply fails then indirectly all those whose incomes are related to agricultural incomes will also find themselves in dire straights.

VULNERABILITY

The major thesis of this essay is that vulnerability to a decline in food supply or to a decline in entitlement is a major causal factor of famine. Furthermore, economic development eliminates famine or reduces the probability of a famine taking place by eliminating or reducing both of these types of vulnerability.

Vulnerability is not a standard economic concept. This is unfortunate since in the analysis of famine, vulnerability is a major determining factor. In standard economics, when we consider essentially exchanges and an exchange equilibrium, we usually also have in mind that there exists a continuity of opportunities. Hence if one opportunity drops out there is another possible opportunity that is as good or almost as good. If one trading partner is no longer available, there is another with whom exchanges could be made which involve almost equal gains by both parties through voluntary exchange. If a job with one employer ceases to be available, there is another one with whom one could make an employment contract which is almost as good. Obviously this general approach implies that the general notion of vulnerability is not significant since it is likely to be extremely small.

Insignificant degrees of vulnerability cease to be the case if small changes in the general situation result in large changes in their consequences. Thus somebody existing on a minimal weight-maintenance diet may find that a reduction in income results in perpetual loss of weight and eventually starvation. This is not to argue that this is precisely how the biology of starvation works. It is only an example of a possible serious degree of vulnerability. A more significant example involves those cases in which suffering some degree of vulnerability leads to an adverse sequence that eventually leads to disaster. For example, a shortfall in food might result in a lower energy level in production, and hence a still lower level of income, and at the next stage a still lower level of food availability, etc. From this point of view, the degree of vulnerability to small changes in a situation could be extremely important.

Essentially, we shall consider two basic types of vulnerability—those which involve vulnerability to the supply factors which determine food availability, and, secondly, vulnerability that results in a reduction in effective demand. This second type concerns vulnerability to entitlement availability.

Consider briefly some of the possible food-supply vulnerabilities. Some of these which influence crop yields are likely to result from natural causes. For instance, they may involve floods, droughts, earthquakes, volcanic eruptions, cyclones, windstorms, river erosion, waterlogging, salinity, crop diseases, crop pests, livestock diseases, etc. Some of these disasters may occur suddenly. Others may happen very slowly. The latter is especially true of the type which involves gradual soil erosion such as dealing with river erosion, water salinity, changes in the water table, excessive withdrawal of ground and surface water, and so on. The main point here is not simply the consideration of a number of possible events which reduce crop yields. The main point is that these events may be more or less important depending on the existing level of the crop yield. If we can define such a thing as a famine level below which famine conditions may be said to exist, then clearly the extent to which current yields are above the famine level is of considerable importance. The closer that actual yields are to the famine level, the greater the vulnerability. Obviously when yields are very much above the famine level, then these various gradual or even sudden natural disasters will have a considerably lower impact and most of them will not result in famine.

The other significant type of vulnerability is that involving entitlements. The major elements concern sources of income. For those who directly earn their income from farming, these vulnerabilites are unquestionably related to food supply. Thus, all of the factors that reduce the size of crops, or crop value, will also reduce income and hence influence the degree of vulnerability. In other words, all those who continue to farm through the famine may nevertheless be vulnerable to famines if there is a shortfall in their crops, or in the value of their crops, so that consumption falls below the famine level. Clearly all other aspects related to farming, such as credit availability, water availability, land erosion, etc. enters the picture.

The availability of land as such may also become a critical factor in determining income. For example, sharecroppers may find that either they cannot rent enough land to grow an adequate crop, or the size of the rents do not leave a sufficient amount for them to have a level of consumption above the famine level. Another element that is likely to be involved is family size. If income cannot grow in proportion to family size as population increases, then falling below the famine level becomes a possibility. In other words, even if in nonfamine years a given family size yields adequate calories, the larger the family the greater the chance of the family getting into the high vulnerability zone.

A great many of those whose income is vulnerable are essentially landless.

They may be landless laborers or those who work in the agricultural sector but outside of agriculture and whose income depends on the expenditures of those who are in agriculture. Artisans of various sorts fit this category. Once again the level of income, and the variability in the income level, will determine the general degree of vulnerability. The above examples in no sense exhaust the number of possibilities but simply illustrates the main general contention: namely, vulnerability depends on income level, assets, and possible variations in income.

Those who are vulnerable would seem to possess three characteristics simultaneously: (1) their current income is quite low and therefore the number of calories above the famine level is also low; (2) they have very few assets to fall back on when income falls; (3) they have very few alternative job opportunities, or other sources of income, or nonincome entitlements.

Another way of looking at all these matters is in terms of the ability to weather an adjustment period in the face of economic adversities. Those who are highly vulnerable will have little capacity to face a long adjustment period required to either supplement their income, or find alternative means of employment, or enable them to settle in some other area. In part, this may simply be a consequence of the initial state of one's health. Thus those who always had an adequate diet may find that they can weather the adjustment period much better than those who are chronically on the margin of famine. Clearly vulnerability and adjustment capacity are two sides of the same coin.

It may be argued that vulnerability is very much related to risk elements associated with economic options. Risk is a well-recognized economic phenomenon and, to a greater or lesser degree, it would be expected that those who make rational choices take the risk element into account. However, risk is not quite the same as vulnerability. High-income individuals with considerable assets may face risk and uncertainty and yet not be vulnerable in the sense that we have discussed the matter. It is true that in choosing their various investments, as well as in choosing their occupation or occupations, they will choose a bundle of activities and assets, some of which may be of a high risk nature. However, since they can choose among a variety of options, they are unlikely to choose a portfolio which will put them anywhere close to a famine position as a result of adverse luck with respect to the outcome of some risky assets. Nevertheless, it is true that those who are vulnerable to famine are in part vulnerable because of a variety of risks and uncertainties against which they cannot insure. Part of the problem is that the asset and options level is so limited that it is impossible for them to self-insure through choosing variety. But insurance of this type does take place in agricultural areas and results in a very high degree of fragmentation in land holdings. Nevertheless, vulnerability does not appear, since these holdings are so limited that a small degree of adversity may push one below the famine level.

Another aspect of the vulnerability phenomenon involves the average food menus consumed and possible substitutions during adversity. The easiest way of looking at this matter is in terms of equivalent primary calories. If a required menu of 2,000 calories is entirely in terms of cereals, with no animal fats or proteins whatsoever, then what is consumed is 2,000 primary calories. However, an equivalent menu of 2,000 calories in terms of only animal food contains 2,000 secondary calories; but in order to produce the secondary calories in the form of domesticated animal calories, something like five- to sevenfold of the primary calories have to be foregone. In other words, the land used to raise the food to feed the animals could produce five- to sevenfold the number of calories in terms of cereal grains. Thus the one who eats domesticated meats is essentially consuming the equivalent of 10,000 to 14,000 primary calories per day. Almost all diets are likely to contain mixtures of primary and secondary calories. However, vulnerability to a reduction in income is clearly less if one is at an income level where one is consuming a high number of secondary calories because in the event of a reduction in income one simply shifts to a higher ratio of primary calories. Thus income loss as such is relatively innocuous in terms of calories as long as substitutions away from meat toward cereal grains are possible. Of course, at higher levels of income other types of substitutions take place as income falls, namely, substitutions away from nonfood uses such as entertainment expenditures, or small luxuries of various kinds, and toward food.

WHY DEVELOPMENT ELIMINATES FAMINES

If we examine what happens when economic development takes place, it is easy to see that the sustained economic development of a country is most likely to work in such a way as to reduce and/or eliminate the risk of famines. Our procedure below will be to discuss briefly the average pattern of economic development, and how the typical patterned changes impinge on reducing the vulnerabilities associated with famine conditions.

Economic development is likely to imply or result in the following phenomena: (1) an increase in output of goods per capita; (2) a shift of labor out of agriculture and into manufacturing and urban-based services; (3) a sustained increase in the capital/labor ratio; (4) an increase in the variety of goods produced and consumed, including the variety of foods; (5) a decrease in the percentage of income spent on food; (6) significant and sustained rural to urban migration so that agricultural labor frequently becomes relatively scarce; (7) an increase in the network of transportation and storage facilities; (8) the gradual and persistent integration of regional markets; (9) increased relations between the economy of the country and the rest of the world; (10) the increased network of governmentally sponsored services to alleviate poverty or the consequences of poverty to some degree.

It becomes evident when we look at our list of changes associated and occurring simultaneously with, or as part of the process of, development that almost all types of vulnerabilities are reduced. The mere increase in outputs and income will almost by itself reduce vulnerabilities, since it allows for some substitutions if income declines. These substitutions are of a kind which are likely to reduce the probability of famine. Thus the various types of phenomena such as urban employment, increased education, increased variety of job skills, are all likely to make it possible for individuals in the event of a loss of one opportunity to take advantage of some other opportunity so as to avoid the worst aspects of previous vulnerabilities. In general, economic development does not eliminate adversity, nor for that matter does it eliminate the possibility of food shortages in some sense; but these risks and uncertainties, and the adversities associated with them, occur at sufficiently higher general levels of food consumption, so that famine as such is not a probable consequence. In other words, most discussion of food shortages in middle-developed countries, or of other types of adversity such as increases in unemployment, involve seriously felt problems to the members of the economy, as well as what people perceive as generally painful adjustments; but the levels adjusted to do not imply starvation. In other words, most economic problems for medium-level developed countries are problems involving the deviation between either a previously achieved level and a temporary lower level of economic well-being, or a deviation from a reasonable aspiration. But this is quite different from the absolute reduction in primary calorie availability which results in starvation.

In addition to the relative vulnerabilities associated with food shortfalls, economic development is likely to eliminate most of the serious entitlement vulnerabilities associated with famines. Since development will be associated with a growing level of assets per family, there is the likelihood of an increasing number of households having something to fall back on when adversity strikes. In addition, even if there is a serious level of unemployment, increasingly unemployment will fall on people who have entitlement cushions as development proceeds. Thus the increasing variety of jobs and other growing cushions to adversity will mean that unemployment will not result in starvation to the extent that it may have in a much less developed economy.

Since entitlement vulnerabilities are in part due to discontinuities in the opportunities available, it would seem clear that there is something wrong with the structure of the economy if entitlement problems are a major cause of famines. If someone loses a job, or other source of income, he or she should be able to find an almost equally good opportunity. The fact that this is not the case suggests that there is something lacking in the supply of entrepreneurial skills, or access to entrepreneurial opportunities. Otherwise, we should normally expect that the discontinuities would be filled. Economic development by widening the nature of the economy, and by increasing variety, is likely to decrease the types of discontinuities that cause entitlement famines.

POPULATION GROWTH AND FAMINE

One of the elements inevitably associated with economic development is population growth. What is the relationship between population growth and the likelihood of famine? A good deal of the writing on this subject appears to suggest that directly or indirectly population growth is a major cause of famine. I suspect that in many cases it would be hard to sustain this position in a careful analysis. It is likely to be extremely difficult under any circumstances to analyze the consequences of population growth. The reason is that the outcome depends on what else is happening in the economy simultaneously.

A given rate of population growth will have one set of consequences if simultaneously the rate of investment and the rate at which innovations are introduced are relatively high, and a very different set of consequences if both of these are extremely low or close to zero. Furthermore, investment and/or the introduction of innovations do not themselves depend on population growth. Hence looking at population growth as an independent variable, we can almost never say with any confidence what the consequences are. But it is possible to make some sensible comments once we constrain to some degree the simultaneous "other happenings."

The clearest cases are those of an economy in which per capita income is quite low, in which the rate of savings is low, and a considerable portion of the agricultural population lives close to the famine threshold. In such cases, the likelihood is that population growth will increase vulnerability to famine. Looking at the matter from a micro viewpoint it seems likely that as a family's size increases the marginal earnings per family member will decline. The larger family is either forced to use the same land more intensively and obtain considerably decreasing returns, or to move to inferior land. This is the classical Ricardian sequence. In either case they are likely to get into a situation in which they are more vulnerable to adversities in agricultural output.

The essential question is how population growth is supported at the margin as per capita income remains approximately constant or close to being constant. Now we can think of a number of scenarios under which there may be delayed consequences which increase vulnerability. Among these are various situations which result in gradually decreasing the fertility of the soil. For instance, accommodating population growth by reducing the amount of land that stays fallow, or reducing reserve acreage under a system of slash and burn agriculture, will yield such results. In each case there is likely to be some sort of exhaustion of the soil as a result. Output vulnerability increases. The same will also be true if population growth is accommodated, knowingly or unknowingly, by the introduction of an innovation which has a similar effect. For example, some superior seeds, or shifting to multiple cropping rather than single cropping, may temporarily increase output but ultimately at the expense of soil exhaustion.

Another possibility involves those changes which result in the increased specialization of agriculture. In other words, a type of commercialization of agriculture takes place under which increased income, at least initially, arises out of the increased value of some specific crop. However, the economy in question cannot control the price of the crop. As a result there may be increased entitlement vulnerability which did not exist under a more variegated agriculture that is somewhat less dependent on price changes.

A third possibility involves a variety of institutional arrangements under which entitlement vulnerability may increase. For instance, the size of land holdings may fall as population increases, or the number of potential share-croppers may increase as land available per sharecroppers declines, or the number of landless laborers increases, and so on. In other words, there may be various configurations which increase the proportion of the population that is vulnerable compared to the ratio prior to the population increase, even though per capita income as such remains constant. Even under situations of per capita income growth, there may also be the possibility of increased specialization so that vulnerability may increase even though the growth per se decreases vulnerability. Of course there are limits to such adverse events. In sum we can see that it is not difficult to imagine scenarios which start with low per capita income and limited growth rates, under which population growth increases the probability of famine. However, we must keep in mind that there are a large number of countries for which this is not the case. That is to say, there still exist many developing countries for whom per capita income growth is significantly above zero so that, on the average, the probability of famine decreases rather than increases as both population growth and development take place simultaneously.

CHRONIC FAMINE, PRODUCTIVITY, AND DEVELOPMENT

The original aim of this essay was to examine famine and its relationship to productivity. However, the research foray I undertook in order to write it led me to the conclusion that this probably was not the wisest option. There are several points that could be made in this area, but they are rather limited in nature. The main points are as follows: (1) Low levels of calories reduce the capacity of labor effort. (2) The most important capacity impairments of low calorie intake are probably psychological ones, especially those involving the will to engage in work and the capacity to concentrate.[3] (3) Beginning at relatively low levels of calorie consumption, calorie intake growth will more than proportionately increase effort capacity. As a result of such generalizations, an argument could be made that, in areas where the consumption level is close to a chronic famine level, increases in food per capita will more than proportionately increase capacity and can contribute significantly to potential output and hence to economic development.

The difficulty with the argument stated in the last sentence is that, while the proposition is true in terms of the possibility of increasing effort, it does not necessarily follow that this will result in increases in output. In other words, the other conditions to take advantage of the increased labor effort simply may not exist. Thus the argument that has to be made is that low levels of calorie consumption imply a hidden available increased effort supply. In circumstances where the inputs are available to use that effort supply, then we can expect dramatic increases in output—that is, output increases more than would be expected simply by looking at capital/manpower ratios. On the other hand, where other inputs are not added at the same time as incomes rise, then the increased effort capacity may simply get lost in some sense. In fact, it may result in visible unemployment whereas previously there was a type of disguised unemployment.[4]

CONCLUSION

The analysis in this paper was built around the interaction between three concepts: (1) food shortfalls, (2) entitlement deficiencies, and (3) the vulnerability status of the household to famine. Entitlement deficiencies may be a cause of famine without food shortfalls, if vulnerability is high, but food shortfalls may also contribute to entitlement deficiencies. In general we argued that the fairly typical patterned changes associated with economic development are likely to reduce or eliminate vulnerability, entitlement deficiencies, and *primary* calorie food shortfalls. The effects of population growth are difficult to analyze without knowing what is happening simultaneously to economic growth inputs. However, where the latter is low it seems likely that population growth increases famine vulnerability. Close to chronic famine conditions are likely to hide a latent labor effort availability because of calorie-effort relations, but the latter may not contribute to growth per capita if other growth inputs are not simultaneously available. From a short-run policy viewpoint, the analysis suggests that simply shipping food to famine areas may be a deficient strategy if entitlement problems are not handled simultaneously.

NOTES

1. A. K. Sen, "Starvation and Exchange Entitlements: A General Approach and Its Application to the Great Bengal Famine," *Cambridge Journal of Economics 1* (1977): 33–59. "Famines" *World Development* 8 (1980): 613–621.
2. Mohiuddin Alamgir, *Famine in South Asia* (Cambridge, Mass.: Oelgeschlager, Gunn and Hain, 1980), pp. 225–239.
3. Ancel Keys, Josef Brozek, Austin Henschel, Olaf Mickelson, and Henry Longstreet Taylor, *The Biology of Human Starvation* (Minneapolis: University of Minnesota, 1950), pp. 714–48.
4. For a more extensive argument of this type, see H. Leibenstein, *Economic Backwardness and Economic Growth* (New York: Wiley, 1957).

ADDITIONAL REFERENCES

Aykrod, W. R. *The Conquest of Famine.* London: Chatto & Windus, and New York: Reader's Digest Press, 1974.
Belli, P. "The Economic Implications of Malnutrition: The Dismal Science Revisited." *Economic Development and Cultural Change* 20 (1971): pp. 1–23.
Franke, R. W. and Chasin, B. H. *Seeds of Famine.* Montclair, N. J.: Allanheld, Osmun, and New York: Universe, 1980.
Leibenstein, H. *General X-Efficiency Theory and Economic Development.* New York: Oxford University Press, 1978.

PART V

The Response to Famine

Despite the terrible fact that most famines today are man-made, it is important to remind ourselves that some segments of society still do respond to the crises of their neighbors. Individuals, voluntary agencies, and governmental organizations do try to cope with the effects of famine, but some are effective while others seem inept.

The contributors to this section reflect the commitment—as well as the frustration—that comes from long experience in dealing with the hungry, poor masses of the Third World.

11

RESPONSE TO FAMINE:
THE ROLE OF THE VOLUNTARY SECTOR

Eileen Egan

A drama about Irish life playing on the New York stage in 1980 shows the main character, an old man losing his job as a gardener when his employer sells the property. At his hour of parting from the garden, the trees, and, above all, the roses that he has nurtured for forty years, the lady of the house presents him with a severance gift that is ludicrously small and tells him that a pension of ten shillings a month has been set up for him.

When Da, the old man, breaks the news to his wife that their monthly pension will be a pittance of about three dollars, she explodes in furious resentment. Da, however, is forgiving.

"They were good to us during the famine," he asserts.

In the year 1943, he is recalling the work of the Quakers, nearly a hundred years earlier. The Society of Friends had played an unforgettable role in one of the worst, if not the worst, famine ever to afflict the European continent. The dread state to which prolonged hunger can bring human beings was viewed by Alexis de Tocqueville on a visit to Ireland. He described those fortunate enough to be received into a poorhouse in Dublin:

> They sit on wooden benches, crowded close together and all looking in the same direction, as if in the pit of a theatre. They do not talk at all; they do not stir; they look at nothing; they do not appear to be thinking. They neither expect, fear, nor hope for anything from life.

A famine seems to sear the imagination of people from generation to generation. It lives on in folk memory, as do the efforts of those who willingly come forward to save threatened lives. When in 1846 the failure of the Irish staple food, the potato, threatened death to a people, it was the Society of

Eileen Egan is director of refugee services, Catholic Relief Services.

Friends who were among the first to publicize the situation. Cecil Woodham-Smith in *The Great Hunger,* points out that it was the "calm, sober evidence of the Quakers" which warned of the need for extraordinary measures to stave off unimaginable tragedy.[1]

The work of the Society of Friends in the Irish potato famine offers a valuable paradigm of the response of the voluntary sector to famine. An analysis will clarify this.

First of all, the Society of Friends warned of impending tragedy. The Irish Friends were joined by the confreres who journeyed from England and brought their experience in feeding the English poor. They told of the approach of the apocalyptic Black Horse of famine so that authorities could take steps to keep at bay the Pale Horse of death. But their warnings were not heeded and apocalyptic events were not staved off.

Food grains could have been diverted to the starving, and fodder to their cows and other farm animals. John Kenneth Galbraith and other economists have pointed out that the Irish Famine was not a complete failure of food supplies, but merely a potato famine. The inhabitants of Ireland, unfortunate enough to be the earliest British colony, had been reduced to a single staple, the potato. Exportation from Ireland of food grains and fodder went on uninterruptedly so as not to interfere with the flow of commerce.

The roads of Ireland, "that most distressful country that ever yet was seen," were filled with pauperized people moving from place to place in search of food. They were described as "dying like rotten sheep," and were buried in mass graves all over the country.

Secondly, when their warnings went unheeded, the Society of Friends set up their own voluntary relief program. At their soup kitchens, food was doled out without "preference on grounds of religion." Nor did they evangelize the starving through food.

Thirdly, they reported to the larger community the almost incredible facts about those condemned to death, reports necessary to the collection of larger resources. They told of the features of children sharpened by hunger until they looked like wizened old men and women, and of the bones of starving people bursting through the flesh.

Fourthly, their work extended far beyond their original intent in response to the unprecedented extremity of suffering, and in this extension they set up a practical organizational network. In January 1847, for example, during the worst days, the Society of Friends were feeding 14,000 of the starving in West Cork, while all official channels reached only 3,000 more. Their work also extended from relief to development when they supplied seeds for the next harvest, all seed potatoes having been consumed.

Finally, in 1849, when the Society of Friends concluded their feeding programs, they "spoke truth to power," pointing out the underlying causes that would have to be rectified so that the people they helped might achieve a measure of justice. Asserting that the problem of relief was "far beyond the reach of private exertion," the Society of Friends stated that government alone could meet the needs of "our suffering fellow-countrymen," and that basic to any eventual betterment in their situation was one enormous program, namely, "the land system of Ireland should be reformed." How much suffering would have been avoided, and how much more peaceful would have been the succeeding history of Ireland if England had heeded the Friends and had begun the task of restitution of land taken from the tillers and awarded to strangers.

POSTWAR VOLUNTARY SERVICES

The response of the Quakers to the sufferings of their compatriots in Ireland has been repeated on behalf of suffering human beings wherever the Society could reach them in their need.[2] Their motivation, recognizing something of the divine in every human creature, originates in the same source as that of the voluntary agency with which I have been associated and of which I am now historian. The first famine we learn about in the New Testament is that which afflicted Jerusalem about two decades after the crucifixion and resurrection of Jesus. We learn that since the believers shared all things in common, they were all hungry together. Paul wrote to the Christians of Corinth urging them to add their gifts to the collection for the hungry of Jerusalem. In those days, when responsibility for the needy rested with the extended family or tribe, the call across borders to people unrelated by blood or tribal ties to relieve hunger was revolutionary. In his appeal, Paul cited the Hebrew Scriptures, "The man who got much had no more than enough, and the man who got little did not go short" (2 Cor. 8:15). This refers to the manna in the desert, with which God mercifully fed the children of Israel. Enough bread from heaven rained down to allay the hunger of the Jews, but only enough for each day's needs was to be taken up. Paul himself took the collected funds to the "suffering saints" in Jerusalem. This example of international help has served the followers of Jesus as the model of religious voluntary help since the first century of our era. Of course, voluntary help has arisen in our pluralist society from other motivations, religious and secular, sometimes from simple human compassion, or human solidarity. We are all aware of the dozens of voluntary agencies, acting out of religious or humanist motivation that have responded to the famine conditions of our time. One of the marks of our American society, as de Tocqueville pointed out, is the habit of taking the initiative to remedy situations without passively awaiting governmental action.

I would offer a few examples from my own experience, examples that parallel the efforts of the Society of Friends between 1846 and 1849.

Catholic Relief Services was founded during World War II to help civilian victims during wartime and to participate after hostilities in the rescue and rehabilitation of survivors. Programs of aid for France, Italy, and Germany were readied as efforts adjunctive to larger governmental and intergovernmental efforts. A particular concern of the agency became the nationless, chiefly Poles, Balts, and Eastern Europeans, who had been dragooned into the Greater Reich as slave laborers in factories and fields. At the Yalta Conference, and later in the original articles of agreement of the United Nations Relief and Rehabilitation Administration (UNRRA), citizens of the various nations were to be repatriated to their home countries with dispatch. The Soviets were particularly anxious to have their own nationals handed over to them. They worked out secret agreements with British and American officials to have Soviet citizens returned by force, at gunpoint.

The Western Allies were left with more than a million and a half Eastern Europeans who refused repatriation to countries now in the Soviet sphere. These were the "displaced persons." The Poles were aware that the eastern half of their nation had been ceded to the Soviet Union at Yalta and that many of their co-nationals had been earlier deported to Siberia and Asiatic Russia.

The recusants were gathered into camps under the control of UNRRA and the Allied military. The camps, scattered about Germany and Austria, were former school buildings, military barracks, battered hotels, and even horse stables. The Soviet Union, a founding member of UNRRA, was able to enter the camps at will and gather lists of inmates. There was heavy pressure on the American and British Allies to use every method to have these displaced persons return to life under the new regimes running their countries. Propaganda films were produced. One of them, "Polska Vas Vita," "Poland Invites You," showed a repatriation train returning to western Poland. Each returnee was seen receiving an enormous sack of food. When the train arrived at the Polish border, it was greeted with flag-waving and singing Poles. It was a well-staged operatic scene. Trains were "at the ready" to take large numbers of displaced persons. UNRRA prepared the enormous sacks of food in a gigantic "Operation Carrot" to promote voluntary repatriation. The response was minimal.

The Western Allies were unwilling to use on the Balts, Poles, and other Eastern Europeans the same brutal methods that had been used on the Russians, so many of whom had committed suicide when they were delivered by trickery to the Soviet military. Allied leaders devised another method. They would close the DP camps during the spring of 1946. Near-famine conditions already afflicted the destroyed landscape of Germany. The mass expulsion of over 15,000,000 ethnic Germans into rump Germany had brought increased hunger to a land where hunger looked out from every eye. The expellees who had been deprived of their home places by the decision of the Allies at Potsdam were made the responsibility of decimated German social and welfare organizations. The displaced persons were living by the life-line of supplies reaching the DP camps. To cut this life-line would mean that they would be exposed to death by hunger or, in despair, would take the sacks of food and climb aboard the repatriation train. We are talking of famine, and while it may be argued that postwar Europe was not afflicted by wholesale famine, there were indeed pockets of famine. The nationless, unprotected displaced persons threatened to become one such pocket.

What could the intervention of the voluntary sector accomplish when all the might of the Allied Powers was intent on achieving their purposes, if not by outright force, then by stealth? The decision to close the DP camps had been made secretly and was learned by voluntary agencies only through an unofficial leak reported by an American news agency in Germany.

First of all, as the Quakers had warned about the need for prior action in Ireland, Catholic Relief Services and other agencies had warned about the dilemma of many Eastern Europeans when the war would end. Catholic Relief Services had sent personnel and supplies to camps of Poles in Mexico, the Middle East, and Africa during the war years. These Poles had been deported to Siberia during the operation of the Hitler-Stalin Pact and had been freed from the Gulag only after Hitler's attack on his old ally. These displaced persons had vowed never to return to Soviet domination. Escapees from other Baltic and other Eastern European nations had expressed the same conviction.

The warnings were not heeded and the Allies hoped to dispose of the troublesome Balts and Eastern Europeans in a speedy manner. Allied leaders could claim that if the displaced persons suffered, it would be by their own choice, since plentiful food awaited them at a nearby UNRRA depot, as well as free transportation to their homelands.

The second stage of voluntary help was that of relief, the provision of supplementary food and clothing to the displaced persons in their camps. The third stage was to report to the larger community the situation of the displaced persons, and to enlarge the network of aid to them by a staff that operated out of offices in such cities as Frankfurt, Munich, Bremen, and Salzburg. But such aid was trifling if the eventual fate of the displaced persons were still in jeopardy.

In the spring of 1946, the Fourth Session of the UNRRA Council was held in Atlantic City. A resolution was offered to remove from the DP camps the 150 liaison officers still maintained by the London-based Polish Government in Exile. This would mean that the displaced persons would receive only news and advice from the political officers of the Soviet-sponsored Polish regime.

The head of Catholic Relief Services, Patrick O'Boyle, later cardinal in Washington D.C., attended the UNRRA Council as an observer, as I did. I approached the head of the British delegation to ask if the leak about the imminent closing of the DP camps was based on fact. I told him that our agency could hardly credit it, since we had staff members in the camps. They would surely have known of such a plan and would have informed the headquarters office.

The delegation head, the late Sir George Rendel, disagreed: "If hundreds of these camps were to be closed, it is conceivable that the only way to do it would be without any warning at all. The writer of the news release indicated that he got wind of it only through an unofficial leak."

He then added pointedly, "There is absolutely nothing you can do by remaining at this UNRRA Session. It is your own government that must be approached if you feel it necessary to overturn this decision."[3]

In his own diplomatic way he had confirmed a plan that would have had the effect of forcible repatriation without the need to send GIs and British soldiers with guns and truncheons.

Then came the step of "speaking truth to power." O'Boyle left the UNRRA Council Session, armed with a memorandum that I had prepared with the help of the late James J. Norris, assistant executive director of Catholic Relief Services. Upon O'Boyle's insistence, he was received by the then Secretary of State, James F. Byrnes. According to Byrnes, the camp closing order would achieve a good end result, namely that a million and a half men, living in idleness, would be forced to work, either for the rebuilding of Western Europe or of their own homelands. The secretary was unaware that many of the DPs were women, also deported for slave labor. It was obvious that the secretary was taking into consideration neither the human rights of displaced persons, the right of asylum and freedom of choice, nor the realities of the death-in-life endured by so many in West Germany.

When O'Boyle returned to the Catholic Relief Services offices, he received reports from staff people in Germany, and communicated again with the office of the secretary of state. This time, the realities of the situation were spelled out. The agency was ready to give full publicity to the camp closing plan and to the hardships it would inflict on innocent people. The State Department had been unprepared for a public outcry in advance of the carrying out of the order. The secretary of state asked O'Boyle to return to Washington for further consultations. O'Boyle continued to "speak truth to power," urging respect for basic human rights. Like many another agency in the voluntary sector, Catholic Relief Services had become the voice of the voiceless, the embassy of the stateless. At this consultation, the secretary of state seemed to see aspects of the displaced persons situation of which he had been unaware, especially the political "fall-out" among Polish-Americans and other American citizens of Eastern European origin. Shortly thereafter, our agency was informed that the decision to close the DP camps had been reconsidered and reversed. Nothing about the matter was broadcast to the press by either the government or by our voluntary agency. The displaced persons had been saved by action of the voluntary sector.

Of course, the saving of the displaced persons camps posed to the voluntary sector the immense challenge of over a million and a half persons who could not remain where they were, who had to be resettled so that they could put down new roots in receiving countries around the world. At this point, the various religion-related voluntary agencies put their energies at the service of their own faith groups, one of the few instances in which religious lines were drawn. Catholic Relief Services reached out into the American community for help. Under the direction of Edward E. Swanstrom, who succeeded O'Boyle as director of Catholic Relief Services, a network called the National Catholic Resettlement Council was formed. Displaced persons could be admitted to the United States only when home and job assurances were provided by American citizens. A vast "paper war" for human happiness began when assurances were matched with the desires and skills of the DPs.

After UNRRA was succeeded by the International Refugee Organization, the voluntary sector was utilized to the fullest in helping displaced persons become not only "new Americans," but "new Canadians" and "new Australians." The voluntary agencies introduced training and language courses in the DP camps to prepare the DPs for resettlement. After the great migration of DPs had almost ended, it was only those broken in mind and body who were left to the cold, trapped existence of the camps. Then the voluntary sector, through such agencies as Catholic Relief Services, Church World Service, and International Rescue Committee, located protective placements for the last and the least. I cite this to indicate two particular qualities of voluntary effort, namely concern for continuity of service and mindfulness of small pockets of distress or famine.

VOLUNTARY SERVICES TO THE FAMINE-STRICKEN

On numerous occasions, American voluntary agencies have decided on joint action on behalf of the famine-stricken. Early in the 1950s the United States possessed something the world had never seen, so great a mountain of surplus foods that the storage bill of a million dollars a day became a drain on the national budget. The war-time challenge of provisioning the largest army ever transported from one nation to a wide perimeter around the globe had catapulted American farmers into spiralling productivity. The U.S. government, to avoid dislocation of the nation's farming community, purchased what was produced in excess of home needs. Following that, the government pledged itself to parity payments for the production of its farmers. Wheat was piled into tent-like enclosures in the Southwestern deserts and loaded into the hulls of the "ghost fleet" from Puget Sound to Virginia's James River. In 1950, widespread famine impelled the Indian government to appeal for American food aid. India's interventions at the United Nations, however, were so often at variance with U.S. positions that haggling in Congress held up action on famine relief. A cartoonist reacted to the situation with a drawing of a corpulent American legislator lecturing the world from the top of a mountain of grain, while a skeletonized Indian looked up disconsolately from the grain-mountain's base. His caption was "The Sermon from the Mount." Various voluntary agencies, including my own, made representations on behalf of the hungry people of India. The arguments were removed from political considerations and were based on human need and human solidarity. Eventually, the Indo-American Wheat Agreement was signed, and a few of us who had spoken on behalf of the famine-stricken were asked to be present at the White House for the signing.

When the powdered milk and other items were stored for so long a period that they were in danger of spoilage, they were released to voluntary agencies for distribution through their relief programs overseas. The first item released was powdered milk. In the years after World War II, millions of refugees, in addition to the displaced persons, were in need of urgent help if they were to survive. A huge "Operation Milky Way" came into being. In three years, between 1950 and 1953, twenty-one American voluntary agencies distributed 215,000,000 pounds of powdered milk to the famished of the world, in particular to areas like Hong Kong. The area commonly called Hong Kong comprises not only the granite rock of that name but surrounding territories covering 391 square miles. The millions of destitute refugees who descended on the colony after the 1948 change of regime on the mainland were helped to survive by unremitting and back-breaking efforts of American voluntary agencies, in particular Church World Service, Lutheran World Relief, and Catholic Relief Services. My own agency during the worst years operated 159 feeding centers and produced noodles which the Chinese could cook on their tiny stoves.

The Chinese refugees saved in those years of hunger have through their industry made Hong Kong a prosperous center of world trade.

The American voluntary agencies, forty-four of them, in daily contact with a hungry world, saw the mountain of surplus growing while the poor overseas received only what was in danger of spoilage. All forty-four of the agencies joined in a statement to their government. It was entitled "The Moral Challenge of Our Abundance." It urged changes in the U.S. government regulations by which food was released for voluntary agency distribution: first, that "danger of spoilage" be removed as the reason for the sharing of food, and secondly, that all foods in storage, including butter, grains, and beans, be released to the needy overseas through the channels of the voluntary sector.

The statement said in part: "It is seldom that a happy circumstance prevails whereby an abundance of surplus of stocks and burdensome storage costs are diminished with proportionate expansion of understanding and good will; whereby an exchange is effected which in a sense translates material gifts into spiritual realities among peoples."

It ended with the assertion: "In their programs of giving aid on the basis of need without reference to creed or other factors, these agencies have made an immeasurable contribution to peace in areas of tension and unrest."

The fact that Quakers, Lutherans, Episcopalians, Jews, Catholics, humanists, and other groups representing the religious, cultural, and ethnic pluralism of the American people, could unite in such requests eventually had its effect on Congress. In succeeding legislation, the "danger of spoilage" criterion was omitted, and a wide variety of surplus foods was released for overseas feeding programs by a broad spectrum of people-to-people agencies. Taxes raised from these constituencies made possible the building up of the food stockpiles, so it was a logical step for the people-to-people agencies to call on the stockpiles for programs of human survival and social peace.

Again, the voluntary sector was fulfilling its role as the voice of conscience to governments on behalf of voiceless and threatened members of the human family.

The program of concessional sales (meaning lower than market prices) of American grains and other foodstuffs to nations overseas under a regulation known as Title I of the Agricultural Act (Public Law 480) reduced the mountain of surpluses. In addition, there was another regulation, Title II, through which voluntary agencies could draw on precious stocks for ongoing relief and emergency feeding programs. This became known as "Food for Peace," and its chief spokesman in Congress was the late Senator Hubert H. Humphrey. The voluntary agencies applauded his impassioned speech in which he supported their aims. "At a time," he said, "when we are signing one alliance after another for military security and military assistance, I ask our government not to tell the people of the world that we do not know what to do with our surpluses of food and fiber. If we do that, we are not going to build peace or strength; we are going to build hatred, fear, and resentment."

With the needs of the Asian refugees in mind, much of the wheat channelled there was eventually processed into pearl-like beads similar to rice. This wheat product, already parboiled, resembled the bulgur wheat used from biblical times. Where flour would have been unusable, because of lack of fuel and ovens, the rice-like wheat product could be boiled like rice over tiny twig or kerosene fires. Its availability for overseas feeding was a result of reports and tests performed by voluntary agency groups in Hong Kong, Korea, and other concentrations of the poor in Asia. Following the hostilities in Korea, four million refugees from north of the 38th parallel fled into South Korea where hundreds of villages were no more than charred ruins and fifty-three out of fifty-five towns and cities were bombed into almost total destruction. Starvation, like a horizon-to-horizon vulture, filled the sky over the homeless of Hong Kong, Korea, and Bengal. It is easily forgotten that at the partition of India in 1947, 16,000,000 men, women, and children were displaced. Into the province of West Bengal, India, came at least 4,000,000 while about 1,000,000 fled into East Bengal, later Bangladesh.

The hungry newcomers could have brought total catastrophe to already denuded areas unless the link had been made between them and the mountains of food in the United States. This link was maintained not only through governmental programs but also through emergency mass feeding efforts by people-to-people agencies which reached the pockets of starvation. It was a quiet work, conducted day-in-and-day-out by unknown Americans (along with uncounted thousands of volunteers) who knew that they were involved not only in the initial survival of victimized people but their eventual entry into the productive life of the human family.

THE "FOOD FOR PEACE" PROGRAM CONTINUED

On the twentieth anniversary of the "Food for Peace" program, Mother Teresa of Calcutta happened to be in Washington, D.C. At the invitation of Senator Hubert Humphrey, she came to his hearing on world hunger. She sat with the representatives of American voluntary agencies who had been associated with her in feeding and rehabilitation programs for the poorest of the poor of humankind. Church World Service, Lutheran World Relief, CARE, United Jewish Appeal, and Catholic Relief Services flanked her. Mother Teresa thanked Americans for not turning away from the world's hungry and for their continuous generosity. She took the occasion to point out that recent cutbacks in "Food for Peace" had caused the elimination of whole categories of needy recipients, including destitute families and the poor in institutions. The dying destitutes gathered from the streets of Calcutta and brought to the Pilgrim's Hostel at the Kali Temple in Calcutta were among those deprived of supplementary food.

The dread word "triage" entered common parlance, a word invented, it is said, on the battlefields of World War I. Triage meant a three-fold division of the wounded into those who need immediate care and seem to have a chance of survival, those not so seriously injured who might survive without immediate treatment, and those who seem to have no chance of survival. For the last category, the awesome decision had to be taken to allow them to perish so that scarce medical attention might be saved for those who might survive. This word might also be applied to nations whose drive towards destitution might be deemed irreversible. Many of us remember that a high American official called violence-gutted, cyclone-prone, heavily-populated Bangladesh a "basket-case."

Mother Teresa might be seen as a finger pointing to human need and to the urgent duty of mobilizing efforts to meet that need. At times the presence of a voluntary agency in a setting of immense need is also hardly more than a finger pointing to unmet needs, a finger that helps move the minds of human beings from their private concerns to the concerns of others whose very survival may be at stake—even though they may live half-a-world away.

By the time of the Congressional hearing led by Senator Humphrey in the mid-seventies, the mountain of U.S. surplus grains was no more. American grain had entered world markets as more and more countries bid for each harvest. No longer were reductions in food surpluses welcomed as a part of an effort to reduce storage costs or relieve the country of food in danger of spoilage. "Food for Peace" was re-examined critically and its continuation, even in reduced form, was due to the voluntary sector's ability to translate into public programs the moral concerns of an aroused and aware citizenry. The whole experience of "Food for Peace," its original organization, its use of voluntary agencies, its achievements and its shortcomings, were of crucial importance in a world where decisions as to who would or would not receive foods might be decisions as to who would live and who would die.

CONTINUED VOLUNTARY SERVICES

In the face of continuing hunger and threats of famine around the world the executive officers of the three major religion-related agencies, Protestant, Catholic, and Jewish, have called upon their followers to meet the challenge of hunger "precisely in terms of the faith we confess . . . at the Passover

Seder and the eucharistic meal." Men, women, and children were asked to fast from food, particularly meat, and donate what they saved to the poor of the world through the appropriate agency. The new approach presented not only the moral challenge of the mountains of surplus foods stockpiled by their taxes, but also the moral challenge presented by the abundant life of ordinary Americans as contrasted with the daily struggle for survival of other segments of the human family. Catholic Relief Services, which conducts its annual appeal for funds during Lent, a time of penance and voluntary fasting, inaugurated "Operation Rice Bowl" by which each family would set aside for the hungry the daily amount saved by restraint in eating habits. Someone has called this approach "living more lightly on the earth."

By such mindfulness of others' needs, the agencies in question have over decades provided about three-fourths of all overseas aid and have been able to respond to successive instances of famine.

Having been immersed in so much of the world's suffering, and having seen at first hand the effects of the mercilessness of war, these agencies fear that their works of mercy may again be swallowed up in the merciless activity called war. A rare example of voluntary help to the famine-stricken at the height of a war occurred in Africa.

When Nigeria exploded in civil war, and the oil-rich seceding province was progressively cut off from food supplies, a spokesman for the Lagos government, defending the food blockade, stated, "All is fair in love and war and starvation is a method of warfare." This brutal concept has been applied in all the wars of the twentieth century, but it has rarely been so baldly enunciated. European church groups joined American church-related agencies in gathering foods for the blockaded province then called Biafra, and inhabited chiefly by the Ibo people. The only way to break the blockade was to send in planeloads of food which would fly in such a way as to avoid anti-aircraft fire. The planes had to land at night on makeshift airstrips lit fleetingly by hand-held torches to avoid becoming the targets of bombing raids. Joint Church Aid was the name given to an operation that proved costly to the lives of pilots and others engaged in the dangerous enterprise. In a unique program, the voluntary sector insisted on performing the works of mercy for those caught in the merciless activity we call war. War has always been an activity that calls for the reversal of every work of mercy from feeding the hungry to giving drink to the thirsty. War, in the instance of Biafra, was successfully invaded by the very quality it aimed to eradicate for the duration, mercy.

In a few months, the blockaded people were able to use the food supplies to set up well over a thousand feeding stations, in schools, town centers, and clinics. Pictures were brought out of long lines of children, already showing the listless eyes, the distended stomachs, and shrunken chests of advanced starvation. Kwashiorkor had turned their hair a grisly white-orange. Countless of these children were saved, but for some it was too late. Tales reached us of children simply wasting away, of little ones so weak that they could not be roused by food or medicaments. Some did not know that they were simply slipping into death. The older ones knew. We were told of a young girl, thirteen, who had seen death all around her and knew that she could not escape it. She cried for two weeks until she, too, died. I feel sure that a hundred years after the Nigerian conflict when the causes are hazy and emotions have cooled, the descendants of survivors will remember the men and women of many nations who "were good to us during the famine."

When the war in Nigeria ended, some of us felt that a new page of history had been written, in that the larger church bodies were joining the Quakers in insisting on feeding civilians, especially the children, on both sides of the conflict. Such a position calls for voluntary agencies and their personnel to refrain from taking or enunciating a political position, no matter what the provocation. Politics has been described as "the process by which power is acquired and exercised in human affairs."[4] Having spent my life with a voluntary agency I have come to a conviction that may be controversial. Let others deal with politics and the question of power. To reach the victimized on both sides of a conflict, the voluntary agency must be free from the temptation to, and the alliance with, power. Only in that way can it, and its meaningful work, be sufficiently distanced from the centers of power to "speak truth to power" on behalf of the helpless, the voiceless, the nationless who are most vulnerable to prolonged hunger and famine conditions. Such undeviating dedication to human need across conflicts is the true soil of reconciliation and eventual peace. Need it be emphasized that the concept, expressed by some, of using food as a weapon is anathema to those who hope by their efforts to build bridges of peace among segments of humankind?

Most of the examples mentioned in this essay deal with the man-made causes of famine, especially war and its aftermath—changes of regime and political persecution. It would seem that our century is marked by man-made famines. Do I need to mention the famine that actually began to take hold when 10,000,000 people fled in 1971 from what was then East Pakistan into one of the poorest provinces of the world, Bengal, India? A quarter of a million of them camped at the doors of Calcutta, threatening to drown the already over-burdened city in their mass misery. From Calcutta, all along a winding border, the millions were herded into temporary shelters, some only covered with a tarpaulin against monsoon rains. Though a small percentage died from cholera and related diseases, the vast majority were snatched from death by a massive influx of life-saving foods and medicines. The voluntary sector distinguished itself in halting the famine, working side by side with United Nations and governmental agencies.

Fortunately, almost all the refugees from what became Bangladesh were returned to their homes at the end of hostilities. How much the massive exodus and internal dislocation accompanying the 1971 hostilities contributed to the 1974 famine is a matter for analysis.

SELF-HELP PROGRAMS

There have been instances where the voluntary sector helped to prevent famines through early intervention and flexibility of program. Such was the case in Bihar in the late 1960s. It was already announced as the "Bihar famine" when voluntary agencies joined with official organizations in providing hundreds of "Food-for-Work" projects. The food transfers were from U.S. stocks. Speedy action prevented this "famine" from entering the history books and had three results: it prevented the depopulation of drought-scourged rural areas; it obviated the expected rush of the starved to the nearest cities; it left Bihar with a far better infrastructure in roads, safe wells, and hygienic facilities than before the threatened famine.

Such activities of the voluntary sector illustrate a particular quality which voluntary agencies bring to the international scene, namely, the power to reach into the smallest communities. This is accomplished without the mounting of a bureaucracy, which is not only costly but which takes time to mount and dismantle. Another program for Bihar's villages exemplifies the fact that though food transfers are often the most obvious response to famine, there are other responses allied to long-term development. To commemorate the hundreth anniversary of the birth of Mahatma Gandhi a special project was inaugurated. It was in the spirit of Gandhi's question, "Recall the face of the poorest and most helpless man whom you may have seen and ask yourself if the step you contemplate is going to be of any use to him: will he be able to gain anything by it?" Food-for-Work projects were established in the poorest Bihari villages for the purpose of constructing wells. Not only was food provided for the men and women who gave full- or part-time work to the project but the necessities for constructing over two thousand wells were supplied by Catholic Relief Services.

The thousands of small self-help projects aided in India, Korea, the Middle East, Africa, and Latin America are so small and specific that they do not capture the news media. In general they are initiated by local groups which have the energy and initiative but lack even minimal extra resources. These projects are captured, with details and photographs, in the communications prepared by the voluntary agencies for the people on whom they rely for their existence. Many such projects reach out to those who are far removed from important governmental and intergovernmental programs, namely women's projects, and in particular, projects dealing with rural women. Each of the American religion-related voluntary agencies has a section linking American women's organizations with women around the globe.

Rural women are the key to food production in the developing world. Help to them is vital since they are the ones who, along with their families, are first affected by food shortages and incipient famines. In response to requests from a women's group in Kenya, funds were supplied to improve the water supply. Responding to requests from women in the Cameroons, Bolivia, and Honduras, help has been transmitted from the National Council of Catholic Women for food-producing cooperatives.

Similar woman-to-woman programs have been established in remote corners of the globe through women's groups affiliated with the other religion-related voluntary agencies.

Dealing as they do with so many millions of the world's peoples who are constantly on the edge of starvation, the American agencies in the voluntary sector are especially aware of the crucial importance of all international efforts toward justice and the redress of inequalities that may ward off catastrophe and bring us into a somewhat better world by the year 2,000. They see the effects of pollution, of desertification, and of high fuel prices and economic exploitation on the world's vulnerable peoples. They realize the need for a new world economic order, the need to lessen North-South economic disparity and the overarching imperative of ending the military confrontation between East and West.

THE MAN-MADE REFUGEE DISASTER AND FAMINE

Since our century has been called the century of the refugee, I would propose that the uprooting of peoples, the man-made disaster of the refugee, be examined as a causative factor, both now and in the future, for famine and near-famine conditions. Dr. Cahill reports on the dire need in Somalia, one of the world's poorest countries, which is beggared by the influx of about 1,500,000 people from the Ogaden region. Here the Inter-Church Response for the Horn of Africa is rushing medical and other aid from Church World Service, Lutheran World Relief, and Catholic Relief Services. We also need to think of the future of over a million refugees from Afghanistan facing an unknown period of their lives in Pakistan's windswept northwest frontier and the desert-like areas of Baluchistan province. Even here, an Inter-Aid Committee of Protestants and Catholics is able to supply tenting and quilts for thousands of refugees.

The case of Somalia should awaken the world to larger dangers in Africa, for it is in Africa that famine conditions may arise where the countries of first asylum for close to six million refugees are desperately poor themselves. I refer to the hundreds of thousands who have fled from Chad and Equatorial Guinea to Cameroon, from Rwanda and Burundi to Tanzania, from Uganda to the Sudan. These are only a few examples.

In Asia, the spectacle of the "boat people" taking to the sea in frail, overcrowded craft, moved receiving nations to open their doors to speedy immigration. Thailand, Malaysia, Hong Kong still have their packed camps of Vietnamese and Cambodians. Cambodia itself became a nation of famine when about 4,000,000 of its people were internally displaced by a regime that was intent on making all things new according to orthodox Marxism. The regime of Pol Pot took literally the dictum of the Communist Manifesto to remake society "by the forcible overthrow of all existing social conditions." The voluntary sector could not enter a Kampuchea sealed off from all outside help until Pol Pot's hold on the countryside was weakened. It was discovered that a near million of the internally displaced were massing at the Thai border, prevented from overrunning the country by Thai forces. The massive food supplies stocked at the Thai-Kampuchean border, which had not been allowed to reach the famine-stricken, were now utilized in a bizarre life-saving operation. Catholic Relief Services sent in food-laden trucks at soft spots in the border, distributing the foods and then darting back for more. Month after month, the compassionate program was conducted on a "hit-and-run" basis until agreements were made with the succeeding regime to bring in regular supplies not only by truck through land entries but also by sea. This is one example from countless others of the creativity and flexibility of voluntary agencies in meeting hunger, a flexibility hardly available to governments.

The voluntary agencies will need such creativity and flexibility, as well as the increased generosity of their constituencies, if they are to deal with the continuing food scarcity caused by the uprooting of peoples. The uprooted can live only by the compassion of others, and if this compassion grows cold, their fate may be sealed.

In our century, it has become evident, the famines arising from natural disasters have been less threatening to human survival than those that were man-made. Even those famines that seemed to be natural disasters were exacerbated by the actions of human beings.

The first famine I discussed was due not only to the natural disaster of a potato failure but to the deprivation of other grains by a colonial power. It was this latter factor that made it a true famine. Similarly, the 1943 Bengal famine, which took at least 2,000,000 lives was related to a lowered rice crop, but also to war conditions which caused requisitioning of rice and of the delivery craft needed to supply communities on Bengal's waterways.

The famine conditions caused by drought in the countries of the African Sahel would seem to be a natural disaster without man-made input, although historians point to the dislocation of food production caused by colonial insistence on peanut production as a remote cause. Even here, the voluntary sector played its role not only of emergency relief but of prior warning. For years preceding the drought, representatives of Catholic Relief Services were helping local villagers to dig deeper wells in the face of an impending water shortage. One representative, Roger Bisson, working out of Ouagadougou, Upper Volta, one of the Sahelian countries, focused on well digging for so many predrought years that he conscientized the agency personnel on the matter. Even after the worst of the drought was over, nomads whose flocks perished needed aid either to obtain new animals or to find ways to put down roots in resettlement programs. This cannot be a mass program, since particular life-styles and customs are involved. A similar problem has arisen as regards the nomads of the Ogaden region, whose survival depends on goat and camel herds that are no more.

Admittedly, the very real possibility of future famines is one to produce alarm, but the alarm should not be so great as to preclude or paralyze action by the voluntary sector. Too many near-famines have been averted, too much help has been channelled to near-famine situations to allow for any feeling of helplessness.

SUGGESTIONS FOR THE FUTURE

First, those in the voluntary sector must exert their duty as citizens. They need to share their expertise and experience in meeting human need and to provide the "distant early warnings" which they gather from involvement in the lives of vulnerable human beings rather than from bloodless statistics. Their moral imperative of responding to hunger and famine should be reflected in the use made of their taxes. Need it be said that voluntary agencies question the size of the so-called "defense budget" (of their own nation as well as the global budget) in relation to the budget allocated for human needs? The $500 billion expended on arms and armies absorb the scientific skills, the technical expertise, and the human power that could help avert the tragedy of famine. We may consider a small example. We hear of the fantastic achievements of intelligence through satellites. Could not such intelligence technology be harnessed to predicting drought and consequent famine and shared through UN agencies?

Secondly, there is the task of joining with those voluntary efforts aimed at arousing citizen awareness and action. "Bread for the World," an outstanding citizens' movement, provides information on world hunger and a channel through which citizens may undertake common advocacy action vis-à-vis their government. The Hunger and Global Security Bill promoted by Bread for the World is a project of immense possibilities for a less hungry future. One of its provisions calls for commitments by governments receiving U.S. food aid to take specific steps toward meeting the basic needs of their people.

Thirdly, as citizens of the planet, as members of the human family, those in the voluntary sector should urge on their government the duty to provide in each budget adequate funding for such irreplaceable agencies as the Office of the UN High Commissioner for Refugees. This agency has earned recognition as an objective instrument in serving purely humanitarian ends. Its limitations are linked to inadequate funding. Other UN agencies meeting far-flung human needs are the World Health Organization, the World Food Program, and UNICEF, the UN International Children's Emergency Fund. Urgently necessary for international food security is the establishment of an International Grains Arrangement with larger emergency reserves and a food financing facility.[5] In the opinion of many, the agency that needs stronger leadership and more effective funding is the one agency that should study and alert the world community to the preconditions of famine. This is the UN Disaster Relief Organization, UNDRO. The period of the eighties may be the time for some concerned member nations to champion the expansion of UNDRO so that it may take on tasks presently dispersed among a variety of specialized agencies. Should not UNDRO become a responsible expression of the international community with regard to future famines and a more effective tool for humankind's survival?

Such actions by the voluntary sector are surely related to the larger issues of reduction of tension and preservation of peace in the world.

At the same time, the voluntary sector must continue to be alert to protect the most threatened members of the human family, to speak truth in defense of human rights, and, in particular, of that right threatened by famine, the right to life itself. Such protection can hardly be left to governments or intergovernmental bodies. This protection calls for uninterrupted watchfulness and uninterrupted generosity on behalf of those in far places whose only tie is a common humanity. Need it be pointed out that, just as the Society of Friends helped save the dying Irish without reference to creed, so the agencies in the voluntary sector help those whom they can reach on only one basis, the basis of need. Loyalty, in this age so endangered by mass hunger and mass incineration by the thermonuclear threat, cannot be less than to the human species as a whole. The uninterrupted generosity may call for sacrifice, for a simpler life-style on the part of the donors, so that, as the Bible put it, "Those that had much had no more than enough, and those that had little did not go short."

Each aid and development agency in the voluntary sector derives its impetus from its own tradition. An underlying tradition of mercy is common to all the major religious groups, perhaps more specifically enunciated in some, including the Judaeo-Christian, the Islamic, and the Buddhist, than in others. The ethical thrust of humanism also leads to compassionate aid across boundaries. The impetus to respond to famine that moves the supporters of my own agency is a simple one. Feeding the hungry is a basic work of mercy, and it is the merciful who may obtain mercy from the All-Merciful. We are the followers of him who told us in the parable of the Last Judgment, "I am the hungry one," and to meet any famished human being is to meet none other that Jesus himself.

NOTES

1. Cecil Woodham-Smith, *The Great Hunger: Ireland 1845–1849* (London: Hamish Hamilton, and New York: Harper & Row, 1963; London: New English Library, 1974).

2. Howard Kershner, *Quaker Service in Modern War* (Spain and France, 1939–1940) (New York: Prentice-Hall, 1950), *inter alia*.

3. "Strangers and Pilgrims," manuscript on the world's refugees by the author of this essay.

4. Peter L. Berger and Richard J. Neuhaus, *Movement and Revolution* (New York: Double-day, Anchor, 1970).

5. *North-South: A Program for Survival*, Report of the Independent Commission on International Development Issues under the Chairmanship of Willy Brant (Cambridge, Mass.: Massachusetts Institute of Technology Press, 1980), Annex 1, Summary of Recommendations.

12

BENEVOLENT CHAOS:
THE CAPACITY OF INTERNATIONAL
AGENCIES IN DISASTERS

Stephen Green

COORDINATING UN RELIEF:
AN ORCHESTRA WITH MANY CONDUCTORS

The Charter of the United Nations, signed in June 1945 barely one month after the demise of the Third Reich, reflected sparse concern for social and developmental matters. The delegates to the conference in San Francisco were understandably mindful of the need for an international organization that would "save succeeding generations from the scourge of war." UNICEF, the most famous of UN social organizations, was founded to assist the war-afflicted children of Europe, and would have gone out of business in 1949 if a Pakistani delegate had not stood up in the General Assembly and shamed the representatives of industrialized countries, reminding them of the plight of children in what we now call the Third World.

There is no mention at all in the UN Charter of responsibility for disaster relief. But by the early 1970s, UN involvement in development matters generally, and food production specifically, in disaster-prone developing countries had raised expectations in the international community for an effective UN response in major disasters. In 1971, the General Assembly created a special UN organization to coordinate international responses to disaster—the United Nations Disaster Relief Office, or UNDRO.

Things have not worked out for UNDRO quite as they were planned ten years ago. By 1971, the Food and Agriculture Organization (FAO) had for fifteen years been the leading UN agency in all food-related matters, a World Food Program had been established primarily to handle food redistribution in emergency situations, and UNICEF had already coordinated UN efforts in several major humanitarian relief operations.

Stephen Green is former regional coordinator, U.N.D.P., UNICEF, and OXFAM.

So UNDRO, created without any operational capacity or mandate at all, created as a "focal point in the United Nations system for disaster relief matters," found that its first task was not relief coordination, but inter-agency diplomacy. To be sure, there have been other problems in UNDRO's first decade. Leadership has been lacking. There has been a constant struggle for funding and staff. And that marvelous UN personnel system licked its lips at the sight of a brand new UN agency and proceeded to dump upon it the dregs of numerous national and international civil services.

But the major problem with UNDRO over the past ten years is that it has been all dressed up with no place to go. Member states of the UN and the other UN agencies simply cannot agree what its role should be. The enabling resolution which created UNDRO empowers it to "mobilize, direct and coordinate" the activities of other UN agencies in disasters, and envisions other roles related to disaster prevention and pre-disaster planning.[1] In practice, UNDRO has spent much if not most of its efforts obtaining more staff and money, defining and re-defining its responsibilities vis-à-vis other UN organizations, and trying to find out what, in a given disaster, the many private, governmental, and UN agencies are in fact doing. When you're scrambling to survive, you don't have much time to "mobilize, coordinate and direct."

In 1950, the General Assembly created the Office of the High Commissioner for Refugees (UNHCR) to provide "international protection" for refugees.[2] Over the years, the term "protection" has been increasingly broadly defined. In addition to legal protection, UNHCR had to provide the victims of conflict or political oppression with the means to exist until repatriation or resettlement could be achieved. As larger and larger numbers of refugees had to be maintained for longer and longer periods, UNHCR relief work has melded into responsibility for rehabilitation and reconstruction phases. In 1980–1981 in Somalia the UNHCR program has had to include long-term agriculture, small-industry, water-supply, and other developmental projects for over a million people forced to build more or less permanent communities from the sand up in the middle of desert savannah.

The concept of protection has come a long way indeed. But this leaves UNHCR with some of the same problems that UNDRO has. Both organizations lack the operational (i.e., technical and logistical) capacity to perform effectively the tasks now expected of them.

UNICEF often gets stuck with the job which UNDRO and UNHCR haven't the ability to do—and UNICEF doesn't want it. The United Nations Children's Fund long ago ceased working uniquely for children. For years now—and certainly during the two so-called "development decades"—UNICEF has become in effect the United Nations Social Development Program. In disaster after disaster—both natural and conflict-related—UNICEF has been reluctantly dragged into a major relief involvement. There have been exceptions, as in Cambodia, where UNICEF has thrust itself forward. But the Fund's field manual and overall policy clearly state that UNICEF will undertake no emergency responsibility for which any other organization has a capability.

There, of course, is the rub. UNICEF has a large supply division with purchasing and shipping experience worldwide. It has a water-supply section, a transport-maintenance section, and the largest and most effective public information division of any UN agency.[3] Most importantly, UNICEF has all these functions permanently established and staffed in a wide network of field offices throughout the developing world. When the victims of war cross the border or when drought sends people to the roadsides and towns in search of food, it is rare that UNICEF isn't asked to play a major role in the relief operation.

There are several other UN agencies which became involved in international disasters, but their capacities are more specialized than those of the three aforementioned organizations. WHO, FAO, the World Food Program, UNDP, and even UNESCO provide assistance related to their special fields of development work. Occasionally, as was the case with FAO and the World Food Program in the Sahel, one of these agencies is designated by the Secretary General to exercise a coordinative and administrative function for the whole UN family of agencies, but this happens only rarely.

This brings us around to the basic problem with the UN's relief capacities—the lack of leadership. For reasons I have indicated, UNDRO cannot "orchestrate" the several UN agencies likely to be involved in a major disaster. The Office of the Secretary General could, but doesn't do so. More often than not, the UN agencies fall into their respective roles by circumstance more than design, with the result that they wind up re-inventing the wheel.

To give one brief current example, UNICEF, which has had a long-standing transport management operation in Somalia, has not been asked to assist with the logistics of the refugee relief operation there. UNHCR, with little experience in this field generally and none in Somalia, has started its own separate transport program over the last year. Why? Because there was no aegis for supra-agency coordination. The government of Somalia, which of course manages the overall refugee relief operation, does not know the UN system and did not know whom or what to ask for.

THE RED CROSS SYSTEM: INTERNATIONAL FIRST AID

The Red Cross system is the other entity which truly qualifies as an "international agency" operating in disaster situations. To the degree possible the International Committee of the Red Cross (ICRC), a uniquely Swiss organization, concentrates on legal protection for the victims of conflict, leaving to the League of Red Cross Societies the job of coordinating material relief. The League is the central federating organization, the hub if you will, of some 122 national Red Cross Societies. The League regularly provides a variety of emergency assistance fully as diverse as that supplied through the UN system. But increasingly, the League is asked by disaster-affected countries to provide experienced personnel to form the backbone of a major relief operation. With 122 national Red Cross Societies to draw upon, the League can do this far more quickly and efficiently than can the UN system.

Generally speaking the Red Cross system has an efficient impact on a major relief operation unless the local Red Cross Society in the disaster-affected country is hopelessly dishonest or unprepared, and insists upon managing only the Red Cross portion of the operation. When that happens, the League and/or the ICRC usually apply diplomacy and tantalizing gifts of trucks and communications equipment, mixed judiciously with ominous, oblique references to the local society's responsibilities under the Red Cross Principles and Rules of Relief. Technically, a national Red Cross Society can have its credentials lifted, though this has never yet occurred.

No matter how effective the Red Cross is in a given operation, however, it can only meet a fraction of the needs in a major disaster, and only very short-term needs at that. The Red Cross has neither the access to large government funding nor the "development" expertise to play other than a strictly emergency role. Along with the voluntary agencies, then, it functions essentially as international first aid.

INHERENT PROBLEMS IN THE
INTERNATIONAL DISASTER RELIEF SYSTEM

Certain operational problems in a major relief operation are virtually unavoidable. But for this very reason, we should be able to plan for them and limit their effect on the life-and-death functions of such an operation.

An example is the ad hoc method by which funds, food, and other relief supplies are raised for emergencies. When an earthquake strikes Guatemala or the world suddenly becomes aware of hunger in Nigeria, there is an outpouring of funds, supplies, and equipment from many diverse sources all over the globe. If newspapers have writ the story large in the Federal Republic of Germany, then the German Evangelical Church may have undertaken a large fund-raising campaign for the event. Other churches, and humanitarian organizations of various kinds, friends of Africa or Latin America, businesses with interests in the general geographic area of the disaster, and the newspapers themselves—they may all take up the cause. The FRG Red Cross Society may want to assist. Finally, the FRG Government may decide to assist through its embassy in the stricken or a nearby country. This pattern may be multiplied in dozens of donor countries.

The result is a flood of contributions from a bewildering variety of sources. Some of these groups may be primarily interested in victims who are children, others interested in Protestant Christians. Some may wish to focus on medical needs, others on hunger. Most of these groups will proceed from information about needs in the distant disaster area derived from different sources. Similarly, most of them will want to have people "on the spot," or at least reports from people on the spot about the utilization of *their* contribution.

With a good start like this, it is easy to see how so many relief operations end with delay, waste, and duplication of effort. Such was the case in the Guatemalan earthquake operation, where the vast majority of medicines sent were never even sorted, let alone utilized for the emergency. Some of the notable food items that were brought in were canned cherries and packages of liquid meat tenderizer which, when ingested, created health problems instead of solving them.[4]

As population increases and food deficits grow in developing countries which are disaster-prone, the frequency and extent of international food assistance in emergencies has grown commensurately.

By 1985, the World Food Council projects a net deficit of 85 million tons among developing market (i.e., noncentrally planned) economies, broken down as follows:

Africa	....	-21 million tons
Latin America	....	+ 5 million tons
Near East	....	-20 million tons
Asia and Far East	....	-49 million tons
	TOTAL	-85 million tons

Since grain exports from developing countries do not, from the standpoint of disaster vulnerability in a subsistence-economy population, offset the gross deficit, it is the latter figure which is significant in terms of potential food crises. And the estimates for *gross* deficits in developing regions change the picture somewhat:

Africa	....	-20 million tons
Latin America	....	-10 million tons
Near East	....	-20 million tons
Asia and Far East	....	-50 million tons
	TOTAL	-100 million tons

And large-scale international food assistance is another inherently inefficient aspect of disaster relief. The other "commodities"—medical supplies and equipment, clothing, shelter, sanitary facilities, etc.—are usually provided only one time to any disaster or conflict victim. Sustained feeding, on the other hand, may require a measured, constant supply of bulk food over a period of time.

Any system that cannot plan for, estimate the need for, call forward, purchase, ship, off-load, transport, distribute, and monitor the use of the "one-shot" items is certainly not going to be able to efficiently manage the supply of needed food.

Beyond that, food poses other special problems. Cereal grains, which are the stuff of emergency operations, have a high shelf life and are not recognizable as to their source or point of origin. They are, in other words, a form of hard currency, and are readily divertable to nonrelief purposes.

The need for and provision of food is an emotionally charged, highly political subject in any society, but most particularly in the traumatic conditions surrounding an emergency operation. There is often a temptation on the part of governments in such situations, therefore, to use food or the lack of it, to achieve political purposes. Established regimes and opposition groups are mutually aware of this fact. On the donor side, there are similar political temptations. In the United States, which provides approximately two-thirds of all emergency food aid globally, there is a veritable literature, in past years, that has grown up around the justification and methods of applying U.S. political self-interest to the decisions regarding which food-deficit countries should be allowed to, *(a)* eat or *(b)* starve.[5]

Another pervasive weakness of the international disaster-relief system which is almost too obvious to mention is the very limited administrative resources in Third World nations. To the confusion of the gaggle of agencies which descend upon a disaster-afflicted developing country is usually added the jumbled, perplexed direction of local agencies struggling to come to terms with the tremendously complex logistic, technical, public information, etc. demands of a major relief program. Countries which do not have the human resources to manage on-going development projects are not well positioned to furnish capable administrators for emergency operations.

Civil defense and emergency preparedness are increasingly appreciated as useful concepts in poor, disaster-prone countries with recent, bad experiences, but their ability to act upon those concepts is limited indeed. At the present time, only about one quarter of the disaster-prone developing countries have *in place* the legal structure, staffing, stockpiled supplies, etc. to respond to even the earliest stages of a major disaster. When disasters do occur, and the assignment of people to relief administration becomes absolutely necessary, such dilution is often resented by line government agencies, and even resisted by the usual forms of bureaucratic guerrilla warfare. This is the case right now in the Somalian refugee emergency.

RECENT EFFORTS AT REFORM

In the last six or seven years, international disaster-relief agencies have been so constantly and pointedly criticized that the governments which provide the bulk of the contributions to the system simply demanded reform.

In the early 1970s the worst famine in recorded African history struck across the entire 4,000 mile southern perimeter of the Sahara. Millions of people were affected in vast, inaccessible areas. In the Sahelian countries, local authorities and U.S. and UN relief officials witnessed mass migrations southward and mused about the "encroaching desert." In Ethiopia and Somalia it was worse. Cholera quickly spread throughout the drought zone, killing or contributing to the deaths of a quarter of a million people by late 1973.

Governments in both disaster zones, as well as international relief agencies, were quite unprepared for the scope of these tragedies and they dithered, and dissembled, and finally mounted what were popularly called "relief" operations. In fact, the natural elements worked their way on those caught by drought and communicable disease in the Sahel and Ethiopia until the rains came and epidemics ran their course. It was primarily changes in the weather that brought relief. Such food and material goods as were finally mobilized arrived too late to prevent most of the dying. After further delays and diversions in port cities, these were distributed in what were actually rehabilitation, not relief, programs.

Naturally, these huge cataclysms were newsworthy events and attracted senior foreign correspondents from many parts of the world—but particularly from Europe, the United States, and other parts of the West which traditionally provide international disaster relief. The correspondents who came to report on the disasters per se often stayed to cover another story—the delay and corruption of host governments, and the delay and inefficiency of the giant relief agencies. Hardly anyone was spared; the Red Cross was severely criticized, as were several UN organizations such as FAO, the World Health Organization, and even UNICEF. Bilateral agencies such as USAID and the British Overseas Development Ministry were targeted as well, particularly by their own national news media.

In spite of the negative publicity, over $300 million was raised for Sudano-Sahelian relief in little more than two years. But after it was all over, people in the drought-affected countries began to ask questions.

Several of the regimes in disaster-struck countries began to come under severe internal criticism. In Niger and Ethiopia foment and opposition ultimately led to revolutions which were attributed, in part at least, to those governments' poor performance, or nonperformance, in their respective disaster situations.

But something else arose from the human and material debris of the African famine, something which may ultimately be more important than the ignominious passages into history of Diori Hamani and Haile Selaissie. Even before the tattered lines of victims disappeared in Africa, a process of reform was underway in Europe and particularly in the U.S. that would substantially alter the international disaster-relief system, the relationship between relief and the much larger concern of development assistance, and even, perhaps, the status in international law of certain of the victims of natural disasters.

In five short years from 1974 to 1979 the major international disaster relief agencies were whipsawed from journalistic criticism of individual relief operations, to booklength exposés of patterns of failure, to "private" policy research in which the major relief agencies were themselves (not always joyously) involved, to internal policy studies by donor governments and agencies, and finally, to far-reaching policy and funding changes. The vast majority of this activity took place or was initiated within the United States.

One reason for this uncharacteristic bureaucratic responsiveness was the recurring theme in the studies and hearings on the African disasters of a linkage between major natural disasters on the one hand, and economic, social, and political disruption, on the other. Viewed as "charity," as a logistic and an accounting exercise, disaster relief had never seemed to involve policy questions at all, except "whether?" "how much?" and "how efficiently?" In the early 1970s, however, against a backdrop of region-wide food shortages, plummeting world food reserves, and poverty in the "Fourth World," which appeared untouched by the UN's "first development decade," disaster relief suddenly seemed very much a "high politics" issue. As if to underscore this, the Horn of Africa staggered from famine to revolution to one conflict after another, in a very convincing state of destabilization.

The results came in 1977–1980. In Washington, Congress increased several-fold the funds available for USAID assistance to natural disaster preparedness programs. The State Department issued an eighteen-point action memorandum calling for, among other things, a much more activist posture by U.S. missions overseas in the face of the political problems of (particularly) famine emergencies.[6] The 1977 International Conference of the Red Cross in Bucharest formally approved a resolution allowing the ICRC to offer (with the concurrence of the League) its legal protection services to disaster victims, in instances where relief is being denied for political reasons. In Geneva, UNDRO and the League began joint investigation of the prospects for and possible outlines of an international convention on disaster relief. UNDRO upgraded and expanded its disaster preparedness section. In Holland, the 1977 summer "Hague lectures" at the Academy of International Law were delivered by the UNDP Administrator on the subject of "international rescue operations."

A SECOND LOOK AT "REFORM," PAST AND FUTURE

All of this research and policy-making in the late seventies was very gratifying to those who were involved. It seemed for a while that the major agencies in New York, Geneva, Washington, and elsewhere were really determined that there be no more "Sahels," no more "Nicaraguas," no more "Ethiopias." But in retrospect, the reform process described above amounted to little more than the sensitizing of the major international relief agencies. Real progress toward a responsive worldwide system for disaster assistance is yet to come.

The Cambodian relief operation of 1979–1980 was a coordination nightmare, and politics again prevented timely relief from reaching those most needy. In Somalia in those same years, UNHCR delayed for six months setting up a relief operation for the hundreds of thousands of Ethiopian refugees streaming into that country. When the operation finally was established, with UNHCR in an administrative role and voluntary organizations acting as executing agencies in the field, the UNHCR central office in Mogadiscio was understaffed with inexperienced people. Funding delays for specific projects added to the frustration and confusion.[7] A severe drought, the full extent of which was assessed only after it was having a wide impact on the existing Somali population, has considerably complicated the issue of utilization of grain imported for the refugees.

Taken together, these two disaster operations have indicated the need for much further reform of the international disaster-relief system. I would suggest certain specific areas of concentration:

1. *Preparedness assistance and early warning.* UNDRO and USAID still provide little more than advice and training to governments or developing countries wishing to create a national response capacity. Beyond advice, what is needed is money, transport, communications, and data-retrieval equipment, i.e., the "hardware" of national-disaster preparedness. UNICEF, not UNDRO, should be the UN agency channeling this assistance.

One particular area of preparedness which should receive immediate attention is food-crisis early warning. Existing NOAA-EDIS satellite rainfall-monitoring data are presently wasted, i.e., not sent expeditiously to the line government agencies in developing countries which can act upon this information.[8] UNICEF/FAO and USAID should collaborate in a program that establishes a framework for regular transmission and utilization of this information in regions with chronic histories of food shortages.

2. *Operational capacities for UN agencies.* UNICEF should be designated the leading UN operational agency for natural disasters, and UNHCR for conflict-related disasters. Each agency will need additional staff and funds for the purpose; particular emphasis should be placed upon giving the two organizations the technical staff and resources to actually operate relief and recovery operations, even if this duplicates existing technical resources of other UN development assistance organizations. Why? To ensure the speed, integrity, and continuity through the various phases of each major relief/reconstruction/rehabilitation disaster operation.

3. *Mobile relief-coordination teams.* UNICEF and UNHCR should have teams equipped, trained, and prepared to buttress national government disaster administration when catastrophes occur on the scale of the recent Cambodian and Somalian operations. In "off-peak periods," these teams should administer the new, UN disaster-preparedness hardware assistance programs.

A PROPOSAL FOR INTERNATIONAL RELIEF COORDINATION

UNDRO was a good idea which was propagated in the General Assembly a decade ago with the best of intentions. It just hasn't worked. I have already discussed some of the reasons for this. The totality of UNDRO's failure, however, is fully described in a recent evaluation report done by the Joint Inspection Unit of the UN Secretariat.[9] This is by far the most candid, blunt, negative internal assessment of a UN agency's performance I have ever seen. It is also timely and welcome.

The report, however, has one major fault: it deals with effects and not causes. It is true, as the report says, that UNDRO has not provided leadership to the UN system in international relief operations. It is also true that the Office has in practice had uncertain, tentative relations with other UN organizations, and with the Red Cross, and that it has wasted valuable time "getting organized." Not surprisingly, the JIU report lays the blame for these failures on the wrong doorstep. The primary reason for the continuing disarray of the UN system in dealing with major disasters has been the refusal of the secretary general to get involved.

Technically, the United Nations disaster relief coordinator is supposed to be the personal representative of the secretary general. The exact words of Resolution 2816 which created UNDRO have the coordinator acting "on behalf" of the secretary general and reporting directly to him. In practice, in day-to-day practice, this doesn't happen. UNDRO isn't even in New York, but in Geneva, 3,500 miles away. Over the last ten years UNDRO has basically had to fend for itself, with perfectly predictable results.

Resolution 2816 should be recast by the General Assembly, limiting UNDRO's role to that of being the information focal point for UN humanitarian relief. UNICEF and UNHCR should clearly and finally be given responsibility for relief-operations management, respectively, in natural and man-made disasters. UNICEF, as previously mentioned, should assume primary responsibility for disaster preparedness and prevention assistance.

While UNDRO's scope of work should be limited, its authority should be strengthened. I submit that UNDRO should be in New York, not Geneva. The coordinator should work directly for the secretary general, who should himself manage a standing UN fund for disaster relief. The secretary general personally should deal with the critical first stages of a major disaster relief operation, and thereafter the coordinator, in physical proximity to the office of the secretary general, should be seen to act directly, literally on the latter's behalf.

The secretary general should also personally deal with the political problems of relief. I am referring here to situations in which needed relief is being delayed or misdirected by a government or governments. Only the secretary general has the substance, the prestige to do this.

The United Nations system of agencies will not be effective in major disaster-relief operations until the secretary general takes the humanitarian initiatives which he alone can take. If the answer to this is that the secretary general hasn't the time to become so directly involved in relief operations, then I think his priorities should be altered. In my opinion, there is no field in which the United Nations has lost more opportunities for constructive action, in recent years, than in the field of humanitarian relief.

NOTES

1. General Assembly Resolution 2816 (XXVI) of December 14, 1971.
2. General Assembly Resolution 319A (IV) of December 14, 1950.
3. UNICEF is unique among UN agencies in that it raises funds through direct solicitations to individuals and organizations, as well as governments.
4. Derived from personal interviews with British TV Journalist Jonathan Dimbleby, who covered the earthquake and relief operations for Thames TV. See also *Evaluation of the Guatemalan Earthquake Relief Operation*, United States General Accounting Office, May 1976.

5. I am thinking here particularly of the work of William and Paul Paddock, *Famine 1975! America's Decision: Who Will Survive?* (Boston: Little, Brown, 1967); also Dale Runge, "The Ethics of Humanitarian Relief: A Systemic Relative Evaluation," a paper for the Alfred P. Sloan School of Management, Massachusetts Institute of Technology, 1973; and Garret Hardin's various writings on the lifeboat ethic. The U.S. Central Intelligence Agency had also undertaken several studies on the political and intelligence problems and options in situations of extreme hunger. See, for example, "A Study of Climatological Research as It Pertains to Intelligence Problems," Office of Research Development of the United States Central Intelligence Agency, August 1974.

6. See Department of State Action Memorandum to the Deputy Secretary from the Assistant Secretary for Policy Planning entitled, "Natural Disaster and Economic Development," dated August 2, 1977.

7. For a candid appraisal of the Somalia refugee program, see "An Assessment of the Refugee Situation in Somalia," a staff report prepared for the Senate Committee on Foreign Relations, September 1980.

8. The data are produced by the Center for Environmental Assessment Services of the National Oceanographic and Atmospheric Administration of the U.S. Department of Commerce.

9. "Evaluation of the Office of the United Nations Disaster Relief Coordination" (JIU/REP/80/11), Geneva, October 1980.

13

DEVELOPING A COORDINATED AND COHERENT U.S. GOVERNMENT POLICY

Arthur Simon

As preventive care makes sense in the area of human health, so public policies designed to prevent famines make sense. My father used to say, "It's better to build a fence at the top of the cliff than to put an ambulance at the bottom." Similarly it is better to prevent famines, where prevention is possible, than to wait until the level of starvation requires emergency intervention. Policies designed to prevent famines deserve our first and highest consideration.

FAMINE PREVENTION

Famine prevention requires that long-range needs be addressed. That, in turn, requires that attention be paid to the poverty and chronic malnutrition that usually lurks behind famine. Unfortunately, it is much easier to draw public attention to famine than to the conditions that are apt to result in famine.

The late Barbara Ward, an internationally distinguished development economist, once described the situation in India during the mid-1960s when a famine had become so serious that millions of deaths by starvation seemed probable. Western television crews arrived at strategic locations so that pictures of this tragedy could be beamed into our living rooms. The deaths, however, never reached predicted levels—so the television crews picked up their equipment and left the country. Massive deaths by starvation are covered by the media and stir widespread public interest, but the problems that make a nation such as India vulnerable to periodic famines are seldom considered newsworthy. The U.S. public remains ill-informed about them, and, consequently, our response to them leaves much to be desired. The public learns to think of hunger primarily in terms of famine and to think of the solution to hunger primarily in terms of emergency relief.

Arthur Simon is executive director of Bread for the World.

152

Place against this perception a major conclusion of the Presidential Commission on World Hunger: "The major world hunger problem today is not famine or starvation, but the less dramatic one of chronic undernutrition."

Famine is only the tip of the iceberg. It is the most visible and dramatic aspect of hunger. Below the line of visibility lies the far more pervasive problem of chronic malnutrition, which not only makes people vulnerable to periodic famine, but also, without waiting for famine, causes thousands of deaths each day. By various estimates, 450 million or more persons are victims of chronic malnutrition.

They are undernourished because they are poor.

The link between hunger and poverty (and therefore between famine and poverty) is illustrated by the thirty-one countries listed by the UN Food and Agriculture Organization (FAO) in April 1981 as having abnormal food shortages—a situation that often precedes famine. According to World Bank figures, in 1978 those thirty-one countries, including China, had a combined population of 1.3 billion people, more than 30 percent of the world's population. The same countries had a combined average per capita gross national product (GNP), which is roughly the same as the average income per person for a year, of $215.

The FAO list did not include some countries, such as India and Bangladesh, in which poverty and malnutrition are widespread, because they were experiencing no abnormal food shortages during early 1981. If India and Bangladesh were added, the list would include nearly half of the world's population and the 1978 annual per capita GNP for those countries would average $198. (Averages conceal disparities, it should be noted, making the actual situation much worse for many people than the figures indicate.) By comparison, the per capita GNP in the United States for 1978 was $9,590 or about forty-eight times that of thirty-three countries with conditions that make them especially vulnerable to famine. Nations such as these with extremely limited resources often lack facilities, services, and materials that provide basic opportunities for people. These include roads, transportation, available markets, access to credit, water, and fertilizer, basic health services and—as the FAO list indicates—an adequate supply of food.

The World Bank estimates that more than 800 million people, roughly 20 percent of the world's population, live in "absolute poverty." Robert S. McNamara, who served as president of the World Bank from 1968 to 1981, describes absolute poverty as "a condition of life so degraded by disease, illiteracy, malnutrition, and squalor as to prevent realization of the potential with which each individual is born." Clearly, where that degree of poverty prevails, hunger prevails, as well, and provides a pool of misery from which the next victims of famine are most apt to emerge.

What type of government policies would most effectively respond to the needs of those in absolute poverty? Those policies, in my judgment, stress economic growth that is equitable, self-reliant, environmentally sound, and, if possible, rapid. The policies should, with few exceptions, emphasize a strong agricultural base as the engine of growth, with food production for domestic consumption as its centerpiece. Both agriculture and industry should stress labor-intensive production in order to achieve the maximum employment of labor.

Equitable growth is important because the poor are so easily bypassed by economic gains. Brazil, for example, experienced dramatic economic growth for almost two decades, but the disparity between the rich and the poor became more extreme. Brazil has a higher per capita income than does Taiwan, for example, but in proportion to the population three times as many people living in absolute poverty. Not surprisingly, malnutrition is much more widespread in Brazil than it is in Taiwan.

Self-reliant growth means that developing countries as well as individuals should use their resources and ingenuity to the utmost and avoid inordinate and prolonged dependence on others. Such growth is not set in opposition to legitimate forms of economic interdependence, nor does it suggest that countries should not specialize in areas of comparative advantage or trade with each other.

The rate of growth is not as important as the kind of growth, but the rate of growth can make a big difference. In 1979 the World Bank projected several hypothetical economic growth rates for developing countries as a whole and estimated the impact of each on the number of persons who would be living in absolute poverty by the year 2000. An annual growth rate of 6.6 percent would mean 470 million persons living in absolute poverty by the year 2000, while an annual growth rate of 4.8 percent would mean 710 million in absolute poverty.

An agricultural-led development strategy in poor countries would not only enable people to be better nourished but the agricultural sector could spur the growth of related industries and provide a ready market for products, such as clothes, tools, and furniture, produced domestically. That is the way industrial economies developed in the northern countries, and efforts so far in poor countries to take short-cuts to industrial development have failed impressively.

A labor-intensive approach to both agriculture and industry, at least in the earlier stages of development, is needed so that poor countries can utilize what they have (an abundant supply of labor) rather than what they lack (an abundant supply of money). This approach would help stem the swelling ranks of unemployed and underemployed people.

To these add the importance of poor people overcoming a sense of powerlessness that is rooted in centuries of collective suffering. As long as impoverished people look at life fatalistically or are prevented by others from taking steps that would enable them to improve their circumstances, they will remain powerless—and poor. As they begin to think differently about themselves and are enabled to participate in decisions that affect their futures, they can often move up to at least an improved level of nutrition and poverty.

The United States could do much more than it is currently doing to encourage poor countries to pursue this way out of hunger and poverty. It could do so through enlightened policies regarding aid, trade, and investment, among others. In this connection the major recommendation of the Presidential Commission on World Hunger is instructive: "that the United States Government make the elimination of hunger the primary focus of its relationships with the developing countries, beginning with the decade of the 1980s." It makes a difference whether or not the United States views poor countries primarily from the standpoint of their role in the political struggle between the two superpowers or from the standpoint of the needs and aspirations of people who are struggling for physical survival.

New York Times reporter Alan Riding summed much of this up in a description in Guatemala:

Some 350,000 people, who abandoned their shacks at the bottom of muddy ravines after the fierce February 1976 earthquake, now live in highly visible hovels beside a six-lane highway in Guatemala City. In the countryside, the Indians live in wooden huts with mud floors and no light or water, illiteracy reaches 80 percent, underemployment is chronic, infant mortality exceeds 100 per 1,000 live births, and four out of five children are undernourished. Generations of poor health have caused impaired eyesight and an above-normal rate of mental retardation, while babies are often born with tuberculosis, contracted inside the womb from their mothers. The Indians, according to a recent United Nations report, are as poor as the poorest in Bangladesh, Somalia, or Haiti.[1]

Riding reported that government repression, combined with extreme poverty, was moving politically passive Indians, who comprise 55 percent of Guatemala's population, to turn increasingly to those who see armed rebellion as the solution. The lesson seems clear: when participation of the poor is not permitted and peacefully encouraged, it may take the form of violence. That is why a much more determined effort on the part of the United States to help people overcome hunger and to avoid strengthening governments that resist reforms toward that end would serve the interests both of preventing famine and improving international security.

FOOD SECURITY MEASURES

Related to the question of long-range policies toward overcoming hunger and poverty in the developing countries is the more medium-range question of their food security. Not many decades ago these countries, taken as a whole, were net grain exporters. In the early 1950s their grain imports amounted to scarcely a trickle. But by 1981 their food imports had soared to an unprecedented 96 million metric tons. FAO reports that the trend would lead developing countries to import 185 million tons of grain a year by the turn of the century. The trend is not expected to prevail, however, because a "crash point" would come first. The poorest half of the world cannot continue for long to increase food imports at such a rapid rate. Meanwhile the increases threaten to seriously aggravate worldwide inflation, divert funds that should be used for internal development, and invite catastrophic famines during periods when global food production drops. Lester Brown, president of Worldwatch Institute, warns that food problems may unfold in the 1980s as energy did in the 1970s, and at least some major U.S. companies are investing in food production technologies with that prospect in mind either for the 1980s or 1990s.

Food and population balance in the developing countries
Indexes, 1961-1965 Average : 100

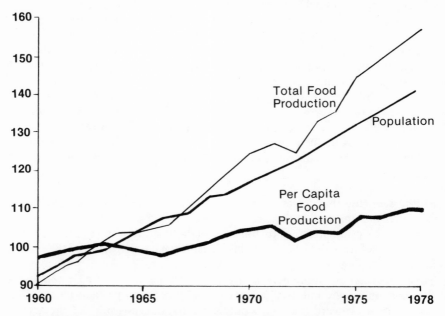

SOURCE: AID data for non-communist countries only.
Presented to Congress for fiscal year 1981.

What is happening is not that food production is falling behind population growth in developing countries as a whole, but that food production is falling behind *market demand*. The graph above indicates a slight increase in per capita food production in the developing countries since the mid-1960s, despite a decline not shown on the graph between 1978 and 1981. That graph would appear to indicate that the problem of hunger is easing, and in some countries that is the case. The graph does not show that many countries, including the continent of Africa as a whole, are steadily dropping in per capita food production. And it does reflect the fact that, as some people in the developing countries become affluent or even less poor, they buy more food. Increases in food production do not necessarily provide more food for those who are malnourished. Sometimes more food produced means more export sales or more food for a minority of persons with rising standards of living, but less food for the rest of the population. In developing countries as a whole the demand for food (that is, effective market demand, reflecting purchasing power) is rising faster than food production. That explains why developing countries are importing food at an alarming rate of increase. And this, in turn, means that unless steps are taken to counter it, the risk of famines on an unprecedented scale is greatly increasing.

A situation similar to the one that developed in the early and mid-1970s and which comes along about once every decade or so could result in such famines. At that time poor harvests in a number of countries led to a decline in world food production. The price of grain skyrocketed. Not only were some poor countries faced with production shortages, but the poor people in many countries were suddenly priced out of the market. Famines, along with an increase in the number of hunger-related deaths even in countries not faced with famine, resulted. If a similar situation developed, say, in the mid-1980s, there would be one striking difference: this time the dependency of developing countries on food imports would be vastly greater, and the likelihood is that many developing countries and many more poor people would be priced out of the market.

Fortunately some steps have already been taken. The first and most important of these was the enactment in 1977 by the United States Congress of a farmer-held grain reserve. Under this reserve, up to 35 million tons of wheat and coarse grain can be stored on farms. Farmers get government loans to pay them for storing the grain, which can only be marketed by the farmers when prices reach a specified level. Farmers pay the loans back when they sell the grain, and they are given incentives to sell when the price reaches designated levels. In this way the reserve serves to stabilize the price and supply of grain both for farmers and consumers to the benefit of both. Although it was tailored for domestic purposes, it also serves informally as an international reserve because the United States controls half of the world's grain exports; therefore stability of price and supply of grain in the United States affects the price and supply world-wide.

Another important step was the enactment in 1980 of a government-owned food security reserve of four million tons of wheat. This reserve functions to insure that U.S. food aid will continue to go to low-income countries with serious food shortages, when the world-wide supply tightens and the price of grain becomes high. In the 1970s the price of grain soared and the money appropriated for U.S. food aid bought less food precisely when it was most needed. The intention of this reserve is to prevent a recurrence of that upside-down response.

A third step was the establishment of a one-half million ton International Emergency Food Reserve administered by the UN World Food Program.

Although small, this reserve could play an important part in meeting localized food emergencies; and if expanded, its role would expand as well.

These three steps add substantially to world food security, but by themselves they do not provide adequate security. Additional steps are urgently needed. These include the following:

1. *Negotiation of a nationally owned but internationally coordinated system of grain reserves.* As of 1981 negotiations were still needed to settle disagreements among developed countries about the price levels, as well as the size of the reserve system and of country shares. Disagreements between developed and developing countries also needed settling. Developing countries have pressed for priority access and preferential price treatment in such a system of reserves, fearing that otherwise commercial reserves would benefit primarily the developed countries, who could buy in large quantities and leave the poor countries last in line.

2. *A food financing facility.* A food fund would compliment reserves of stored food. Food reserves are needed for times when the supply begins to run short and the prices escalate, so that poor countries can count on a supply to provide at least for their most urgent requirements. But during periods when the world supply is ample and the prices moderate, localized food shortages still occur. Under those circumstances it makes sense for a country to borrow money and make purchases on the world market. A food fund would simply expand the idea of reserves and provide additional flexibility. In 1981 a food-financing facility was being developed as a possible operation of the International Monetary Fund.

3. *The varying of food aid to meet recipient country needs rather than donor country supplies.* The four-million-ton U.S. food security reserve of wheat moves somewhat in this direction. Several ways have been suggested for increasing or decreasing food aid on the basis of actual food shortages in developing countries, so that aid responds to the needs of hungry people rather than to the convenience of the assisting countries. But no agreement is yet in sight. As the world's population grows, and as developing countries become increasingly dependent on food imports for survival, additional food-security measures will be required. These will probably include the expansion of existing reserves.

OTHER STEPS

A U.S. policy that would contribute toward food security and famine prevention is one that guards against the political use of food. A small step in that direction was a provision, approved by the U.S. House of Representatives in 1981 and under consideration by the full Congress, to prohibit grain embargoes against countries if such an embargo would cause hunger. By mid-1981 Congress was still considering the measure despite opposition from the administration.

U.S. food aid has been used extensively for political purposes. This abuse reached its zenith in 1974 when most of our Title I food aid went to Indochina to support the war effort—this at a time when famines were occurring in various parts of the globe and total U.S. food aid had shrunk drastically as a result of the soaring price of wheat. More recently, the United States did respond generously to the Cambodian famine. But since 1975, the United States has prevented commercial shipments of food to Vietnam and official U.S. food aid to that country has also been prohibited, despite the fact that Vietnam is a terribly poor country with very serious food shortages. In 1978 Church World Service sent a shipment of 10,000 tons of wheat to Vietnam though the State Department would not cover shipping costs as it normally would for such assistance. In 1981, however, when food shortages were again prompting thousands of people to flee that country, the Mennonite Central Committee could not get an export license from the Department of State in order to ship, at the Mennonites' own expense, 250 tons of wheat to Vietnam. The cutting off of U.S. food aid to Nicaragua the same year also illustrated the use of food for political purposes.

Among other policy measures that could have a significant impact on famine is the question of federal subsidies (or other incentives or restraints) for the use of cropland in the production of ethanol for fuel. Such use of cropland raises at least the possibility that at some point in the future, gas guzzlers of the world could be reducing the supply and boosting the price of food beyond the reach of millions of hungry people.

As the issue of gasohol reminds us, the supply of cropland is not unlimited, and therefore the issue of—and policies regarding—the conservation of land become important as we think several decades or more ahead. The question applies to such diverse but critical factors as the use of cropland for housing or industrial development; soil erosion which, the U.S. Department of Agriculture tells us, is washing away our topsoil at an alarming rate; and the careful development and use of water resources, which may one day dwarf oil as a natural resource in critically short supply.

The sharing of available U.S. photo-satellite information with developing countries for the purpose of detecting early and with some precision impending crop shortfalls might be a major future contribution toward famine prevention and a more prepared response to famines that do occur.

When famines occur, much depends on the attitude, the understanding, and the sense of priorities of persons in leadership positions, starting with the president. There is no substitution for the willingness of leaders to respond. And their will to respond is, in turn, greatly affected by public opinion.

Because public policy does indeed stem to a large extent from the public, each of us has an important role to play in the shaping of such policies. We can, in relatively small numbers, wield an enormous influence on our legislators and other policy makers simply by asking them to adopt specific measures toward the prevention of hunger and famine. The role of Bread for the World in helping to shape the legislation and, through its network of members and links with the churches, to get public support for the two U.S.

grain reserves illustrates that. So does the outpouring of public support for a swift U.S. response to the Cambodian crisis in late 1979. Because more legislation, more policy action, and more awareness at every level is needed regarding the steps that can and should be taken regarding famine and its prevention, the role of citizens in advocating those steps was never more important.

NOTES

1. "Guatemala: State of Siege," *The New York Times Magazine,* August 24, 1980.

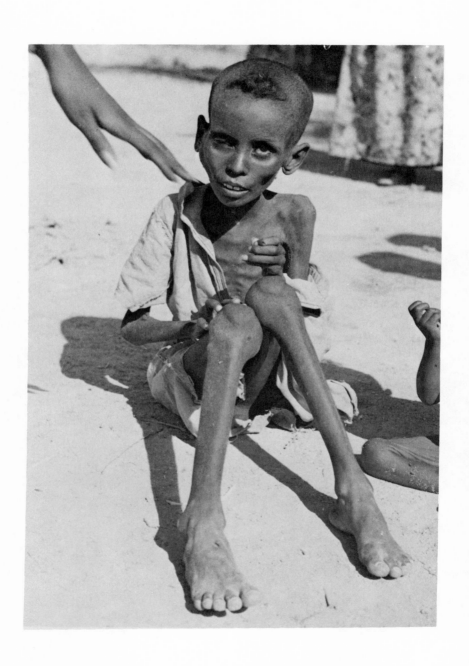

EPILOGUE

It is, perhaps, a common human tendency to defer facing those problems which are either so remote that they can be easily ignored or so massive that they appear irresolvable.

For those of us in the developed countries of the world, famine is, too often, such a problem. But for the poor of the world, it is otherwise. For them, famine is not a problem but a tragic daily deprivation which threatens their most basic human right and is sending so many to untimely graves. And this in a world which has the means, if not the will, to prevent famine.

There is no problem in our world of such urgency, unless it be the madness which makes global nuclear destruction a possibility.

Famine today, like our nuclear capabilities, is man-made and represents a moral crisis which can but should not be ignored. And yet, as is so often the case with problems of enormous scope and centuries-long duration, individuals often feel that there is little they can do to effect change. This sense of helplessness eventually transforms itself into apathy. Our first challenge, then, in the struggle to eliminate famine is to change attitudes on a grand scale so that the problem is seen as one which, together, we can solve.

That has been the purpose of this book. Having read it, you have not found simple answers or even a unified analysis of the problem. But you have heard the views of experts from many fields who have witnessed famine first-hand and are convinced that it need not be.

Children have a way of reducing problems to their starkest terms. When my youngest son, seeing the wasted bodies of famine victims on television, asked, "Why do they let those kids starve?" the answer must be that the "they" is "we" and the question becomes, "Why, indeed?"